WITHDRAWN

PR
6015　　Huxley
U9　　　Essays new and old.
E7
1968

Date Due　　JUL　2000

		JUN	2004
		JUL	09
		JUL X X	2015

ESSAYS NEW AND OLD

ALDOUS HUXLEY

ESSAYS
NEW AND OLD

BY ALDOUS HUXLEY

Essay Index Reprint Series

 BOOKS FOR LIBRARIES PRESS

FREEPORT, NEW YORK

73-128

First published, 1927

LIBRARY OF CONGRESS CATALOG CARD NUMBER:

68-22918

PRINTED IN THE UNITED STATES OF AMERICA

CONTENTS

CONTENTS

Essays New and Old

IN A TUNISIAN OASIS

WAKING at dawn, I looked out of the window. We were in the desert. On either side of the railway an immense plain, flat as Holland, but tawny instead of green, stretched out interminably. On the horizon, instead of windmills, a row of camels was silhouetted against the grey sky. Mile after mile, the train rolled slowly southward.

At Tozeur, when at last we arrived, it had just finished raining—for the first time in two and a half years—and now the wind had sprung up; there was a sandstorm. A thick brown fog, whirled into eddies by the wind, gritty to the skin, abolished the landscape from before our smarting eyes. We sneezed; there was sand in our ears, in our hair, between our teeth. It was horrible. I felt depressed, but not surprised. The weather is always horrible when I travel.

Once, in a French hotel, I was accused of having brought with me the flat black bugs, of whose presence among my bed-clothes I complained to a self-righteous proprietress. I defended myself with energy against the impeachment. Bugs—no; I am innocent of bugs. But when it comes to bad weather, I have to plead guilty. Rain, frost, wind, snow, hail, fog—I bring them with me wherever I go. I bring them to places where they have never been heard of, at seasons when it is impossible that they should occur. What delightful skating there will be in the Spice Islands when I arrive! On this particular journey I had brought with me to every place on my itinerary the most appalling meteorological calamities. At Naples, for example, it was the snow. Coming out of the theatre on the night of our arrival, we found it lying an inch deep under the palm trees in the public gardens. And Vesuvius, next morning, glittered white, like Fujiyama, against the pale spring sky. At Palermo there was a cloud-burst. "Between the Syrtes and soft Sicily" we passed through a tempest of hail, lightning and wind. At Tunis it very nearly froze. At Sousse the wind was so violent that the stiff board-like leaves of the cactuses swayed and trembled in the air like aspens. And now, on the day of our arrival at Tozeur, it had rained for the first time in thirty months, and there was a sandstorm. No, I was not in the least surprised; but I could not help feeling a little gloomy.

Towards evening the wind somewhat abated; the sand began to drop out of the air. At midday the brown curtain had been impenetrable at fifty yards. It thinned, grew gauzier; one could see objects at a hundred, two hundred yards. From the windows of the hotel bedroom in which we had sat all day, trying—but in vain, for it came through even invisible crannies—to escape from the wind-blown sand, we could see the fringes of a dense forest of palm trees, the dome of a little mosque, houses of sun-dried brick and thin brown men in flapping night-shirts walking, with muffled faces and bent heads, against the wind, or riding, sometimes astride, sometimes sideways, on the bony rumps of patient little asses. Two very professional tourists in sun helmets—there was no sun—emerged round the corner of a street. A malicious gust of wind caught them unawares; simultaneously the two helmets shot into the air, thudded, rolled in the dust. The too professional tourists scuttled in pursuit. The spectacle cheered us a little; we descended, we ventured out of doors.

A melancholy Arab offered to show us round the town. Knowing how hard it is to find one's way in these smelly labyrinths, we accepted his offer. His knowledge of

French was limited; so too, in consequence, was the information he gave us. He employed what I may call the Berlitz method. Thus, when a column of whirling sand rose up and jumped at us round the corner of a street, our guide turned to us and said, pointing: "Poussière." We might have guessed it ourselves.

He led us interminably through narrow, many-cornered streets, between eyeless walls, half crumbled and tottering.

"Village," he explained. "Très plaisant." We did not altogether agree with him.

A walk through an Arab village is reminiscent of walks through Ostia or Pompeii. Roman remains are generally in a better state of preservation, and cleaner; that is all. One is astonished to see, among these dusty ruins, white-robed families crouching over their repasts.

Our guide patted a brown mud wall.

"Briques," he said, and repeated the word several times, so that we might be certain what he meant.

These bricks, which are of sun-dried mud, are sometimes, on the façades of the more considerable houses, arranged in a series of simple and pleasing patterns—diamonds, quincunxes, hexagons. A local art which nobody now takes the trouble to practise—nobody, that is, except the Europeans, who, with characteristic energy, have used and wildly abused the traditional ornamentation on the walls of the station and the principal hotel. It is a curious and characteristic fact that, whenever in Tunisia one sees a particularly oriental piece of architecture, it is sure to have been built by the French since 1881. The cathedral of Carthage, the law courts and schools of Tunis—these are more Moorish than the Alhambra, Moorish as only oriental tea-rooms in Paris or London can be Moorish. In thirty years the French have produced buildings more typically and intensely Arabian than the Arabs themselves contrived to do in the course of thirteen centuries.

We passed into the market place.

"Viande," said our guide, fingering as he passed a well-thumbed collop of mutton, lying among the dust and flies on a little booth.

We nodded.

"Très joli," commented our guide. "Très plaisant." Noisily he spat on the ground. The proprietor of the booth spat too. We hurried away; it needs time to grow inured to Arabian habits. These frightful hoickings

in the throat, these sibilant explosions and
semi-liquid impacts are almost the national
music of the Arabs.

There are in the desert of southern Tunisia
three great oases: Gabes by the sea, a little
north of that island of Djerba which is,
traditionally, the classical Island of the
Lotus Eaters; Tozeur, to the west of it,
some seventy miles inland; and Nefta, fifteen miles west of Tozeur, the starting-point
of the caravans which trade between southern Tunisia and the great oases of the Al-
gerian Sahara, Biskra and Touggourt. These
oases are all of much the same size, each
consisting of some six or seven thousand
acres of cultivated ground, and are all three
remarkable for their numerous and copious
springs. In the middle of the desert, suddenly, a hundred fountains come welling out
of the sand; rivers run, a network of little
canals is dug. An innumerable forest of date
palms springs up—a forest whose under-
growth is corn and roses, vines and apricot
trees, olives and pomegranates, pepper trees,
castor oil trees, banana trees, every precious
plant of the temperate and the sub-tropical
zones. No rain falls on these little Edens—
except on the days of my arrival—but the
springs, fed from who knows what distant
source, flow inexhaustibly and have flowed

at least since Roman times. Islanded among the sands, their green luxuriance is a standing miracle. That it should have been in a desert, with here and there such islands of palm trees, that Judaism and Mohammedanism took their rise is a thing which, since I have seen an oasis, astonishes me. The religion which, in such a country, would naturally suggest itself to me would be no abstract monotheism, but the adoration of life, of the forces of green and growing nature. In an oasis, it seems to me, the worship of Pan and of the Great Mother should be celebrated with an almost desperate earnestness. The nymphs of water and of trees ought surely, here, to receive a passionate gratitude. In the desert, I should infallibly have invented the Greek mythology. The Jews and the Arabs discovered Jahweh and Allah. I find it strange.

Of the three great Tunisian oases, my favourite is Nefta. Gabes runs it close for beauty, while the proximity of the sea gives it a charm which Nefta lacks. But, on the other hand, Gabes is less fertile than Nefta and, socially, more sophisticated. There must be the best part of two hundred Europeans living at Gabes. There is dancing once a week at the hotel. Gabes is quite the little Paris. The same objection applies to

Tozeur, which has a railway station and positively teems with French officials. Nefta, with fourteen thousand Arabs, has a white population of a dozen or thereabouts. A hundred Frenchmen can always make a Paris; twelve, I am happy to say, cannot. The only non-Arabian feature of Nefta is its hotel, which is clean, comfortable, French and efficient. At Nefta one may live among barbarians, in the middle ages, and at the same time, for thirty francs a day, enjoy the advantages of contemporary western civilization. What could be more delightful?

We set off next morning by car, across the desert. From Tozeur the road mounts slightly to a plateau which dominates the surrounding country. The day was clear and sunny. We looked down on the green island of Tozeur—four hundred thousand palm trees among the sands. Beyond the oasis we could see the chotts, glittering in the sun. The chotts are shallow depressions in the ground, at one time, no doubt, the beds of considerable lakes. There is no water in them now; but the soil is furred with a bright saline efflorescence. At a distance, you could swear you saw the sea. For the rest, the landscape was all sand and lion-coloured rock.

We bumped on across the desert. Every

now and then we passed a camel, a string of camels. Their owners walked or rode on asses beside them. The women folk were perched among the baggage on the hump—a testimony, most eloquent in this Mohammedan country, to the great discomfort of camel riding. Once, we met a small Citroen lorry, crammed to overflowing with white-robed Arabs. In the Sahara, the automobile has begun to challenge the supremacy of the camel. Little ten-horsepower Citroens dart about the desert. For the rougher mountainous country special six-wheeled cars are needed, and with caterpillar wheels one may even affront the soft and shifting sand of the dunes. Motor buses now ply across the desert. A line, we were told, was shortly to be inaugurated between Nefta and Touggourt, across two hundred kilometres of sand. In a few years, no doubt, we shall all have visited Lake Tchad and Timbuctoo. Should one be glad or sorry? I find it difficult to decide.

The hotel at Nefta is a long low building, occupying one whole side of the market square. From your bedroom window you watch the Arabs living; they do it unhurriedly and with a dignified inefficiency. Endlessly haggling, they buy and sell. The vendor offers a mutton chop, slightly soiled;

the buyer professes himself outraged by a price which would be exorbitant if the goods were spotlessly first-hand. It takes them half an hour to come to a compromise. On the ground white bundles doze in the sun; when the sun grows too hot, they roll a few yards and doze again in the shade. The notables of the town, the rich proprietors of palm trees, stroll past with the dignity of Roman senators. Their garments are of the finest wool; they carry walking sticks; they wear European shoes and socks, and on their bare brown calves—a little touch entirely characteristic of the real as opposed to the literary East—pale mauve or shell-pink sock-suspenders. Wild men ride in from the desert. Some of them, trusting to common sense as well as Allah to preserve them from ophthalmia, wear smoked motor goggles. With much shouting, much reverberant thumping of dusty, moth-eaten hides, a string of camels is driven in. They kneel, they are unloaded. Supercilious and haughty, they turn this way and that, like the dowagers of very aristocratic families at a plebeian evening party. Then, all at once, one of them stretches out its long neck limply along the ground and shuts its eyes. The movement is one of hopeless weariness; the grotesque animal is suddenly pathetic. And what groanings, what gurglings in the throat, what enormous sighs when their masters begin to reload them! Every additional package evokes a bubbling protest, and when at last they have to rise from their knees, they moan as though their hearts were broken. Blind beggars sit patiently awaiting the alms they never receive. Their raw eyelids black with flies, small children play contentedly in the dust. If Allah wills it, they too will be blind one day: blessed be the name of Allah.

Sitting at our window, we watch the spectacle. And at night, after a pink and yellow sunset with silhouetted palm trees and domes against the sky (for my taste, I am afraid, altogether too like the coloured plates in the illustrated Bible), at night huge stars come out in the indigo sky, the cafés are little caves of yellow light, draped figures move in the narrow streets with lanterns in their hands, and on the flat roofs of the houses one sees the prowling shadows of enormous watch-dogs. There is silence, the silence of the desert; from time to time there comes to us, very distinctly, the distant sound of spitting.

Walking among the crowds of the market-place or along the narrow labyrinthine streets, I was always agreeably surprised by the apathetically courteous aloofness of Arab manners. It had been the same in Tunis and the other larger towns. It is only by Jews and Europeanized Arabs that the tourist is pestered; through the native quarters he walks untroubled. There are beggars in plenty, of course, hawkers, guides, cab drivers; and when you pass, they faintly stir, it is true, from their impassive calm. They stretch out hands, they offer Arab antiquities of the most genuine German manufacture, they propose to take you the round of the sights, they invite you into their fly-blown vehicles. But they do all these things politely and quite uninsistently. A single refusal suffices to check their nascent importunity. You shake your head; they relapse once more into the apathy from which your appearance momentarily roused them—resignedly; nay, almost, you feel, with a sense of relief that it had not, after all, been necessary to disturb themselves. Coming from Naples, we had been particularly struck by this lethargic politeness. For in Naples the beggars claim an alms noisily and as though by right. If you refuse to ride, the cabmen of Pozzuoli follow you up the road, alternately cursing and whining, and at every hundred yards reducing their price by yet another ten per cent. The guides at Pompeii fairly insist on being taken; they cry aloud, they show their certificates, they enumerate their wives and starving children. As for the hawkers, they simple will not let you go. What, you don't want coloured photographs of Vesuvius? Then look at these corals. No corals? But here is the last word in cigarette holders. You do not smoke? But in any case, you shave; these razor blades, now . . . You shake your head. Then toothpicks, magnifying glasses, celluloid combs. Stubbornly, you continue to refuse. The hawker plays his last card—an ace, it must be admitted, and of trumps. He comes very close to you, he blows garlic and alcohol confidentially into your face. From an inner pocket he produces an envelope; he opens it, he presses the contents into your hand. You may not want corals or razor blades, views of Vesuvius or celluloid combs; he admits it. But can you honestly say—honestly, with your hand on your heart—that you have no use for pornographic engravings? And for nothing, sir, positively for nothing. Ten francs apiece; the set of twelve for a hundred. . . .

The touts, the pimps, the mendicants of Italy are the energetic members of a conquering, progressive race. The Neapolitan cabman is a disciple of Samuel Smiles; the

vendors of pornographic post cards and the
sturdy beggars live their lives with a strenu-
ousness that would have earned the com-
mendation of a Roosevelt. Self-help and
the strenuous life do not flourish on the other
shore of the Mediterranean. In Tunisia the
tourist walks abroad unpestered. The Arabs
have no future.

And yet there were periods in the past
when the Arabs were a progressing people.
During the centuries which immediately followed Mohammed's apostolate, the Arabs
had a future—a future and a most formidable present. Too much insistence on the
fatalism inherent in their religion has re-
duced them to the condition of static lethargy
and supine incuriousness in which they now
find themselves. That they might still have
a future if they changed their philosophy of
life must be obvious to any one who has
watched the behaviour of Arab children, who
have not yet had time to be influenced by the
prevailing fatalism of Islam. Arab children
are as lively, as inquisitive, as tiresome and
as charming as the children of the most pro-
gressively Western people. At Nefta the
adult beggars and donkey drivers might leave
us, resignedly, in peace; but the children
were unescapable. We could never stir
abroad without finding a little troop of them

frisking around us. It was in vain that we tried to drive them away; they accompanied us, whether we liked it or no, on every walk, and, when the walk was over, claimed wages for their importunate fidelity.

To provide tourists with guidance they did not need—this, we found, was the staple profession of the little boys of Nefta. But they had other and more ingenious ways of making money. Close and acute observers of tourists, they had made an important psychological discovery about this curious race of beings. Foreigners, they found out, especially elderly female foreigners, have a preposterous tenderness for animals. The little boys of Nefta have systematically exploited this discovery. Their methods, which we had frequent opportunities of observing, are simple and effective. In front of the hotel a gang of little ruffians is perpetually on the watch. A tourist shows himself, or herself, on one of the balconies: immediately the general of the troop—or perhaps it would be better to call him the director of the company, for it is obvious that the whole affair is organized on a strictly business footing—runs forward to within easy coin-tossing distance. From somewhere about his person he produces a captive bird —generally some brightly coloured little creature not unlike a goldfinch.   Smiling up at the tourist, he shows his prize.   *"Oiseau,"* he explains in his pidgin French.   When the tourist has been made to understand that the bird is alive, the little boy proceeds, with the elaborate gestures of a conjurer, to pretend to wring its neck, to pull off its legs and wings, to pluck out its feathers.   For a tender-hearted tourist the menacing pantomime is unbearable.

"Lâche la bête.   Je te donne dix sous."

Released, the bird flaps ineffectually away, as well as its clipped wings will permit.   The coins are duly thrown and in the twinkling of an eye picked up.   And the little boys scamper off to recapture the feebly fluttering source of their income.   After seeing an old English lady blackmailed out of a small fortune for the ten-times-repeated release of a single captive, we hardened our hearts whenever birds were produced for our benefit.   The little boys went through the most elaborately savage mimicry.   We looked on calmly.   In actual fact, we observed, they never did their victims any harm.   A bird, it was obvious, was far too valuable to be lightly killed; goldfinches during the tourist season laid golden eggs. Besides, they were really very nice little boys and fond of their pets.   When they saw that we had seen through their trick and could not be induced to pay ransom, they grinned up at us without malice and knowingly, as though we were their accomplices, and carefully put the birds away.

The importunity of the little boys was tiresome when one wanted to be alone. But if one happened to be in the mood for it, their company was exceedingly entertaining. The exploitation of the tourists was a monopoly which the most active of the children had arrogated, by force and cunning, to themselves. There was a little gang of them who shared the loot and kept competitors at a distance. By the time we left, we had got to know them very well. When we walked abroad, small strangers tried to join our party; but they were savagely driven away with shouts and blows. We were private property; no trespassing was tolerated. It was only by threatening to stop their wages that we could persuade the captains of the Nefta tourist industry to desist from persecuting their rivals. There was one particularly charming little boy— mythically beautiful, as only Arab children can be beautiful—who was the object of their special fury. The captains of the tourist industry were ugly; they dreaded the rivalry of this lovely child. And they were right; he was irresistible. We insisted on his being permitted to accompany us.

"But why do you send him away?" we asked.

"Lui méchant," the captains of industry replied in their rudimentary French. "Lui casser un touriste."

"He smashed a tourist?" we repeated in some astonishment.

They nodded. Blushing, even the child himself seemed reluctantly to admit the truth of their accusations. We could get no further explanations; none of them knew enough French to give them. "Lui méchant. Lui casser un touriste." That was all we could discover. The lovely child looked at us appealingly. We decided to run the risk of being smashed and let him come with us. I may add that we came back from all our walks quite intact.

Under the palm trees, through that labyrinth of paths and running streams, we wandered interminably with our rabble of little guides. Most often it was to that part of the oasis called the *Corbeille* that we went. At the bottom of a rounded valley, theatre-shaped and with smooth steep sides of sand, a score of springs suddenly gush out. There are little lakes, jade green like those pools beneath the cypresses of the Villa d'Este at

Tivoli. Round their borders the palm trees go jetting up, like fountains fixed in their upward aspiring gesture, their drooping crown of leaves a green spray arrested on the point of falling. Fountains of life—and five yards away the smooth unbroken slopes of sand glare in the sun. A little river flows out from the lakes, at first between high banks, then into an open sheet of water where the children paddle and bathe, the beasts come down to drink, the women do their washing. The river is the main road in this part of the oasis. The Arabs, when they want to get from place to place, tuck up their night-shirts and wade. Shoes and stockings, not to mention the necessity for keeping up their dignified prestige, do not permit Europeans to follow their example. It is only on mule-back that Europeans use the river road. On foot, with our little guides, we had to scramble precariously on the slopes of crumbling banks, to go balancing across bridges made of a single palm stem, to overleap the mud walls of gardens. The owners of these gardens had a way of making us indirectly pay toll for our passage across their property. Politely, they asked us if we would like a drink of palm wine. It was impossible to say no; we protested that we should be delighted. With the agility of a monkey, a boy would fairly run up a palm tree, to bring down with him a little earthenware pot full of the sap which flows from an incision made for the purpose at the top of the stem, in the centre of the crown of leaves. The pot, never too scrupulously clean, was offered to us; we had to drink, or at least pretend to drink, a horribly sickly fluid tasting of sugared water slightly flavoured with the smell of fresh cabbage leaves. One was happy to pay a franc or two to be allowed to return the stuff untasted to the owner. I may add here that none of the drinks indigenous to Nefta are satisfactory. The palm juice makes one sick, the milk is rather goaty, and the water is impregnated with magnesia, has a taste of Carlsbad or Hunyadi Janos, and produces on all but hardened drinkers of it the same physiological effects as do the waters of these more celebrated springs. There is no alternative but wine. And fortunately Tunisia is rich in admirable vintages. The red wines of Carthage are really delicious, and even the smallest of *vins ordinaires* are very drinkable.

A fertile oasis possesses a characteristic colour scheme of its own, which is entirely unlike that of any landscape in Italy or the north. The fundamental note is struck by the palms. Their foliage, except where the stiff shiny leaves metallically reflect the light, is a rich blue-green. Beneath them, one walks in a luminous aquarium shadow, broken by innumerable vivid shafts of sunlight that scatter gold over the ground or, touching the trunks of the palm trees, make them shine a pale ashy pink through the subaqueous shadow. There is pink, too, in the glaring whiteness of the sand beyond the fringes of the oasis. Under the palms, beside the brown or jade-coloured water, glows the bright emerald green of corn or the deciduous trees of the north, with here and there the huge yellowish leaves of a banana tree, the smoky grey of olives, or the bare, bone-white and writhing form of a fig tree.

As the sun gradually sinks, the aquarium shadow beneath the palm trees grows bluer, denser; you imagine yourself descending through layer after darkening layer of water. Only the pale skeletons of the fig trees stand out distinctly; the waters gleam like eyes in the dark ground; the ghost of a little marabout or chapel shows its domed silhouette, white and strangely definite in the growing darkness, through a gap in the trees. But looking up from the depths of this submarine twilight, one sees the bright pale sky of evening, and against it, still touched by the level, rosily-golden light, gleaming as though transmuted into sheets of precious metal, the highest leaves of the palm trees.

A little wind springs up: the palm leaves rattle together; it is suddenly cold. "En avant," we call. Our little guides quicken their pace. We follow them through the darkening mazes of the palm forest, out into the open. The village lies high on the desert plateau above the oasis, desert-coloured, like an arid outcrop of the tawny rock. We mount to its nearest gate. Through passage ways between blank walls, under long dark tunnels the children lead us—an obscure and tortuous way which we never succeeded in thoroughly mastering, back to the square market-place at the centre of the town. The windows of the inn glimmer invitingly. At the door we pay off the captains of industry and the little tourist-smasher; we enter. Within the hotel it is provincial France.

For longer expeditions entailing the use of mules or asses, we had to take grown-up guides. They knew almost as little French as the children, and their intelligence was wrapped impenetrably in the folds of fatalism. Talking to an Islamically educated Arab is like talking to a pious European of the fourteenth century. Every phenomenon is referred by them to its final cause—to

God. About the immediate causes of things
—precisely how they happen—they seem to
feel not the slightest interest. Indeed, it is
not even admitted that there are such things
as immediate causes: God is directly responsible for everything.

"Do you think it will rain?" you ask,
pointing to menacing clouds overhead.

"If God wills," is the answer.

You pass the native hospital. "Are the
doctors good?"

"In our country," the Arab gravely replies,
in the tone of Solomon, "we say that doctors
are of no avail. If Allah wills that a man
shall die, he will die. If not, he will re-
cover."

All of which is profoundly true, so true,
indeed, that it is not worth saying. To the
Arab, however, it seems the last word in
human wisdom. For him, God is the perfectly adequate explanation of everything;
he leaves fate to do things unassisted, in its
own way—that is to say, from the human
point of view, the worst way.

It is difficult for us to realize nowadays
that our fathers once thought much as the
Arabs do now. As late as the seventeenth
century, the chemist Boyle found it necessary to protest against what I may call this
Arabian view of things.

"For to explicate a phenomenon," he wrote, "it is not enough to ascribe it to one general efficient, but we must intelligibly show the particular manner, how that general cause produces the proposed effect. He must be a very dull enquirer who, demanding an account of the phenomena of a watch, shall rest satisfied with being told that it is an engine made by a watchmaker; though nothing be declared thereby of the structure and coaptation of the spring, wheels, balance, etc., and the manner how they act on one another so as to make the needle point out the true time of the day."

The Arabs were once the continuators of the Greek tradition; they produced men of science. They have relapsed—all except those who are educated according to Western methods—into pre-scientific fatalism, with its attendant incuriosity and apathy. They are the "dull enquirers who, demanding an account of the phenomena of a watch, rest satisfied with being told that it is an engine made by a watchmaker." The result of their satisfaction with this extremely unsatisfactory answer is that their villages look like the ruins of villages, that the blow-flies sit undisturbedly feeding on the eyelids of those whom Allah has predestined to blindness, that half their babies die, and that, politically, they are not their own masters.

It does not need much perspicacity to see that our Western civilization is not perfect, that it is, indeed, in many respects, repulsive and enormously stupid. But Eastern civilizations have their defects as well. The East is not all theosophy and ancient wisdom, as a great many people seem to suppose; bad smells and imbecility also enter into its composition—and copiously, too! The defects of the East, it seems to me, are graver even than ours. Its merits are in their way as great and, for individuals in the present, perhaps greater; but they promise much less for the future. Moreover, as a matter of historical fact, all that we regard as characteristically Eastern in oriental civilizations, whether good or evil, is rapidly disappearing, to be replaced by the conquering goods and evils of the West. Religious mysticism and bad drains, artistic traditions and horrible superstition, fatalistic resignation and irresponsible despotism—all these admirable and detestable features of Eastern civilization are gradually, but with an ever-increasing acceleration, being replaced by practical materialism and hygiene, the industrial system and modern science, restless dissipation of spirit and efficient government. Our current occidental ideas about the East are already out of date; it is only in backwaters, such as Nefta, and among the uneducated that our East still completely survives. Another hundred years and even Nefta will be Americanized. The thought, it must be admitted, is slightly depressing, and would be much more so if we supposed that America and western Europe were going to remain exactly what they are to-day. I am optimistic enough to believe that, a century hence, Western civilization will have been moulded by the logic of circumstances and the intelligence of man into something of whose presence beneath the palms and beside the jade-green waters of Nefta we shall have no reason to feel ashamed.

THE TRAVELLER'S-EYE VIEW

I COULD give many excellent reasons for my dislike of large dinner-parties, soirées, crushes, routs, conversazioni and balls. Life is not long enough and they waste precious time; the game is not worth the candle. Casual social intercourse is like dram-drinking, a mere stimulant that whips the nerves but does not nourish. And so on. These are respectable contentions and all quite true. And they have certainly had weight with me. But the final argument against large assemblages and in favour of solitude and the small intimate gathering has been, in my case, of a more personal character. It has appealed, not to my reason, but my vanity. The fact is that I do not shine in large assemblies; indeed, I scarcely glimmer. And to be dim and conscious of one's dimness is humiliating.

This incapacity to be bright in company is due entirely to my excessive curiosity. I cannot listen to what my interlocutor is saying or think of anything to say in answer to him, because I cannot help listening to the conversations being carried on by everybody else within earshot. My interlocutor, for exam-

ple, is saying something very intelligent
about Henry James and is obviously expect-
ing me, when he has done, to make some
smart or subtle comment. But the two
women on my left are telling scandalous
stories about a person I know. The man
with the loud voice at the other side of the
room is discussing the merits of different
motor-cars. The science student by the fire-
place is talking about the quantum theory.
The distinguished Irish lawyer is telling
anecdotes in his inimitable professional manner. Behind me a youth and maiden are
exchanging views on love, while from the
group in the far corner I hear an occasional
phrase which tells me that they are talking
politics. An invincible curiosity possesses
me, I long to hear exactly what each is saying. Scandal, motors, quanta, Irish bulls,
love and politics seem to me incomparably
more interesting than Henry James; and
each of these is at the same time more interesting than all the others. Inquisitiveness
flutters hopelessly this way and that, like
a bird in a glass house. And the net result
is that, not hearing what he says and being
too much distracted to answer coherently, I
make myself appear an idiot to my interlocutor, while the very number of my illicit

curiosities renders it impossible for me to satisfy any single one of them.

But this excessive and promiscuous inquisitiveness, so fatal to a man who desires to mix in society, is a valuable asset to the one who merely looks on, without participating in the actions of his fellows.

For the traveller, who is compelled, whether he likes to or not, to pose as the detached onlooker, inquisitiveness is nothing less than a necessity. Ennui, says Baudelaire, is *fruit de la morne incuriosité*. The tourist who has no curiosity is doomed to boredom.

There are few pleasanter diversions than to sit in cafés or restaurants or the third-class carriages of railway trains, looking at one's neighbours and listening (without attempting to enter into conversation) to such scraps of their talk as are wafted across the intervening space. From their appearance, from what they say, one reconstructs in the imagination the whole character, the complete life history. Given the single fossil bone, one fancifully builds up the whole diplodocus. It is an excellent game. But it must be played discreetly. Too open a curiosity is apt to be resented. One must look and listen without appearing to be aware of anything. If the game is played by two people, comments should always be made in some language other than that of the country in which the game is played. But perhaps the most important rule of the game is that which forbids one, except in the most extraordinary cases, to make any effort to get to know the objects of one's curiosity.

For, alas, the objects of one's curiosity prove, once one has made their acquaintance, to be, almost invariably, quite unworthy of any further interest. It is possible at a distance to feel the most lively curiosity about a season-ticket holder from Surbiton. His bald head is so shiny; he has such a funny waxed moustache; he gets so red in the face when he talks to his friends about the socialists; he laughs with such loud unpleasant gusto when one of them tells a dirty story; he sweats so profusely when it is hot; he holds forth so knowledgeably about roses; and his sister lives at Birmingham; his son has just won a prize for mathematics at school. At long range all this is fascinating; it stimulates the imagination. One loves the little man; he is wonderful, charming, a real slice of life. But make his acquaintance. . . . From that day forth you take pains to travel in another compartment.

How delightful, how queer and fantastic

people are, at a distance! When I think of
the number of fascinating men and women I
have never known (only seen and momentarily listened to) I am astonished. I can
remember hundreds of them. My favourites,
I am inclined to think, were those male and
female post-office clerks who lived *en pension*
at the little hotel at Ambérieu where once I
stayed for a week or so, finishing a book.
They were fascinating. There was the old-
ish man, who always came in late for dinner,
wearing a cap—a grim, taciturn fellow he
was; there was the very young boy, not at all
grim, but silent out of pure shyness; there
was the very bright, lively, meridional fellow, who made jokes all the time and flirta-
tiously teased the young ladies; and the three
young ladies, one ugly but tolerably lively,
one rather pretty but limp and chlorotic, and
the third so full of attractive vitality that
she compelled one to think her pretty—such
rolling black eyes, such a smile, such a voice,
so witty! The shy young man gazed like a
calf, blushed when she looked at him, smiled
oxishly when she talked, and forgot to eat
his dinner. Her presence thawed the grim
and grizzled man and roused the meridional
to yet higher flights. And her superiority
was so enormous that the ugly girl and the
chlorotic girl were not in the least jealous,

but worshipped her. It is absurd to be jealous of the gods.

How I adored that party! With what passionate interest I overlooked them from my table in the little dining-room! How attentively I eavesdropped! I learned where they had spent their holidays, which of them had been to Paris, where their relations lived, what they thought of the postmaster of Ambérieu, and a host of other things, all wonderfully interesting and exciting. But not for the world would I have made their acquaintance. The landlady offered to introduce me; but I declined the honour. I am afraid she thought me a snob; she was proud of her pensionnaires. It was impossible for me to explain that my reluctance to know them was due to the fact that I loved them even more than she did. To know them would have spoilt everything. From wonderful and mysterious beings, they would have degenerated into six rather dull and pathetic little employés, condemned to pass their lives drearily in a small provincial town.

And then there were the millionaires at Padua. How much we enjoyed those! It was the waiter who told us they were plutocrats. In the restaurant of the Hotel Storione at Padua there is one special table, it appears, reserved for millionaires. Four or five of them lunched there regularly every day while we were in the hotel. Superb figures they were, and wonderfully in character like millionaires in an Italian film. In an American film, of course, the type is very different. A Hollywood millionaire is a strong, silent man, clean-shaven, with a face either like a hatchet or an uncooked muffin. These, on the contrary, had tremendous beards, talked a great deal, were over-dressed and wore white gloves. They looked like a little party of Bluebeards.

Another of my remembered favourites is the siren we saw at the Ristorante Centrale at Genoa. She sat at a neighbouring table with four men, all desperately in love with her, talking, one could see by the way they listened and laughed, like all the heroines of Congreve rolled into one. One of the men was a Turk and had to have recourse periodically to the interpreter, without whose aid the majority of diners in that polyglot restaurant would be unable to order their macaroni. One—he was old and paid for the dinner—must have been her husband or her lover. Poor fellow, he looked rather glum sometimes, when she addressed herself too fascinatingly to the Turk, who was her principal victim, or one of the other men.

But then she gave him a smile, she lifted her pale blue-grey eyes at him and he was happy again. No, not happy exactly; happy is the wrong word. Drunk—that would be more like it, I imagine. Deliriously joyful on the surface; and within bottomlessly miserable. So we speculated, romantically, at long range. What we should have discovered on a nearer acquaintance I do not know—I do not want to know.

The most uninteresting human being seen at a little distance by a spectator with a lively fancy and a determination to make the most of life takes on a mysterious charm, becomes odd and exciting. One can work up a thrilling emotion about distant and unknown people—an emotion which it is impossible to recapture after personal acquaintance, but which yields place to understanding and consequent affection or antipathy.

Certain authors have exploited, either deliberately or because they could not do otherwise, their spectator's emotion in the presence of unknown actors. There is Joseph Conrad, for example. The mysterious thrilling charm of his characters, particularly his female characters, is due to the fact that he knows nothing at all about them. He sits at a distance, he watches them acting and then wonders and wonders, through pages of Mar-

low's winding narratives, why on earth they
acted as they did, what were their motives,
what they felt and thought. The God's-eye
view of those novelists who really know, or
pretend they know, exactly what is going on
in the minds of their characters, is exchanged
for the traveller's-eye view, the view of the
stranger who starts with no knowledge whatever of the actors' personalities and can only
infer from their gestures what is happening
in their minds. Conrad, it must be admitted,
manages to infer very little; he lacks the
palaeontologist's imagination, has little
power of reconstructing thought from seen
behaviour. At the end of a novel, his heroines are as shadowy as they were at the beginning. They have acted, and Conrad has
lengthily wondered—without discovering—
why they have acted in this particular way.
His bewilderment is infectious; the reader is
just as hopelessly puzzled as the author and,
incidentally, finds the characters just as wonderfully mysterious. Mystery is delightful
and exciting; but it is foolish to admire it
too highly. A thing is mysterious merely because it is unknown. There will always be
mysteries because there will always be unknown and unknowable things. But it is
best to know what is knowable. There is no
credit about not knowing what can be known.

Some literary men, for example, positively pride themselves on their ignorance of science; they are fools and arrogant at that. If Conrad's characters are mysterious, it is not because they are complicated, difficult or subtle characters, but simply because he does not understand them; not knowing what they are like, he speculates, unsuccessfully, and finally admits that he finds them inscrutable. The honesty with which he confesses his ignorance is meritorious, not the ignorance. The characters of the great novelists, like Dostoievsky and Tolstoy, are not mysterious; they are perfectly well understood and clearly displayed. Such writers live with their creations. Conrad only looks on from a distance, without understanding them, without even making up plausible hypotheses about them out of his imagination.

He differs in this respect from Miss Katherine Mansfield, another writer who takes the travellers'-eye view of human beings. For Miss Mansfield has a lively fancy. Like Conrad, she sees her characters from a distance, as though at another table in a café: she overhears snatches of their conversations—about their aunts in Battersea, their stamp collections, their souls—and she finds them extraordinary, charming beyond all real and knowable people, odd, im-

mensely exciting. She finds that they are
Life itself—lovely, fantastic Life. Very
rarely does she go beyond this long-range
café acquaintanceship with her personages,
rarely makes herself at home in their flat
everyday lives. But where Conrad bewilder-
edly speculates, Miss Mansfield uses her
imagination. She invents suitable lives for
the fabulous creatures glimpsed at the café.
And how thrilling those fancied lives always
are! Thrilling, but just for that reason not
very convincing. Miss Mansfield's studies
of interiors are like those brilliant palaeonto-
logical reconstructions one sees in books of
popular science—the ichthyosaurus in its
native waters, pterodactyls fluttering and
swooping in the tepid tertiary sky—too ex-
citingly romantic, in spite of their air of
realism, to be quite genuine. Her characters
are seen with an extraordinary brilliance and
precision, as one sees a party of people in
a lighted drawing-room, at night, through an
uncurtained window—one of those mysterious significant Parties in Parlours of which
we read in *Peter Bell:*

> Some sipping punch, some sipping tea,
> And all as silent as could be,
> All silent, and all damned.

One sees them for a moment, haloed with
significance. They seem fabulous (though

of course, in point of actual fact and to those
sitting in the room with them, they are nothing of the kind).   Then one passes, they disappear.   Each of Miss Mansfield's stories is
a window into a lighted room.   The glimpse
of the inhabitants sipping their tea and
punch is enormously exciting.   But one
knows nothing, when one has passed, of what
they are really like.   That is why, however
thrilling at a first reading, her stories do not
wear.   Tchekov's do; but then he had lived
with his people as well as looked at them
through the window.   The traveller's-eye
view of men and women is not satisfying.   A
man might spend his life in trains and restaurants and know nothing of humanity at
the end.   To know, one must be an actor as
well as a spectator.   One must dine at home
as well as in restaurants, must give up the
amusing game of peeping in at unknown
windows to live quietly, flatly, unexcitedly
indoors.   Still, the game, if it is kept as an
occasional diversion and not treated as the
serious business of life, is a very good one.
And on a journey it is your only travelling
picquet.

ACCIDIE

THE coenobites of the Thebaid were subjected to the assaults of many demons. Most of these evil spirits came furtively with the coming of night. But there was one, a fiend of deadly subtlety, who was not afraid to walk by day. The holy men of the desert called him the *daemon meridianus;* for his favourite hour of visitation was in the heat of the day. He would lie in wait for monks grown weary with working in the oppressive heat, seizing a moment of weakness to force an entrance into their hearts. And once installed there, what havoc he wrought! For suddenly it would seem to the poor victim that the day was intolerably long and life desolatingly empty. He would go to the door of his cell and look up at the sun and ask himself if a new Joshua had arrested it midway up the heavens. Then he would go back into the shade and wonder what good he was doing in that cell or if there was any object in existence. Then he would look at the sun again and find it indubitably stationary, and the hour of the communal repast of the evening as remote as ever. And he would go back to his meditations, to sink,

sink through disgust and lassitude into the black depths of despair and hopeless unbelief. When that happened the demon smiled and took his departure, conscious that he had done a good morning's work.

Throughout the Middle Ages this demon was known as Acedia, or, in English, Accidie. Monks were still his favourite victims, but he made many conquests among the laity also. Along with *gastrimargia*, *fornicatio*, *philargyria*, *tristitia*, *cenodoxia*, *ira* and *superbia*, *acedia* or *taedium cordis* is reckoned as one of the eight principal vices to which man is subject. Inaccurate psychologists of evil are wont to speak of accidie as though it were plain sloth. But sloth is only one of the numerous manifestations of the subtle and complicated vice of accidie. Chaucer's discourse on it in the "Parson's Tale" contains a very precise description of this disastrous vice of the spirit. "Accidie," he tells us, "makith a man hevy, thoghtful and wrawe." It paralyses human will, "it forsloweth and forsluggeth" a man whenever he attempts to act. From accidie comes dread to begin to work any good deeds, and finally wanhope, or despair. On its way to ultimate wanhope, accidie produces a whole crop of minor sins, such as idleness, tardiness, *lâchesse*, coldness, undevotion and "the synne of worldly sor-

row, such as is cleped *tristitia*, that sleth
man, as seith seint Poule." Those who have
sinned by accidie find their everlasting home
in the fifth circle of the Inferno. They are
plunged in the same black bog with the
Wrathful, and their sobs and words come
bubbling up to the surface:

> Fitti nel limo dicon: "Tristi fummo
>   nell' aer dolce che dal sol s' allegra,
>   portando dentro accidioso fummo;
> Or ci attristiam nella belletta negra."
>   Quest' inno si gorgolian nella strozza,
>   chè dir nol posson con parola integra.

Accidie did not disappear with the monas-
teries and the Middle Ages. The Renaissance was also subject to it. We find a
copious description of the symptoms of
acedia in Burton's *Anatomy of Melancholy*.
The results of the midday demon's machina-
tions are now known as the vapours or the
spleen. To the spleen amiable Mr. Matthew
Green, of the Custom House, devoted those
eight hundred octosyllables which are his
claim to immortality. For him it is a mere
disease to be healed by temperate diet:

> Hail! water gruel, healing power,
> Of easy access to the poor;

by laughter, reading and the company of un-
affected young ladies:

> Mothers, and guardian aunts, forbear
> Your impious pains to form the fair,
> Nor lay out so much cost and art
> But to deflower the virgin heart;

by the avoidance of party passion, drink, Dissenters and missionaries, especially missionaries: to whose undertakings Mr. Green always declined to subscribe:

> I laugh off spleen and keep my pence
> From spoiling Indian innocence;

by refraining from going to law, writing poetry and thinking about one's future state.

The Spleen was published in the thirties of the eighteenth century. Accidie was still, if not a sin, at least a disease. But a change was at hand. "The sin of worldly sorrow, such as is cleped *tristitia*," became a literary virtue, a spiritual mode. The apostles of melancholy wound their faint horns, and the Men of Feeling wept. Then came the nineteenth century and romanticism; and with them the triumph of the meridian demon. Accidie in its most complicated and most deadly form, a mixture of boredom, sorrow and despair, was now an inspiration to the greatest poets and novelists, and it has remained so to this day. The Romantics called this horrible phenomenon the *mal du siècle.* But the name made no difference; the thing was still the same. The meridian demon had good cause to be satisfied during the nineteenth century, for it was then, as Baudelaire puts it, that

> L'Ennui, fruit de la morne incuriosité,
> Prit les proportions de l'immortalité.

It is a very curious phenomenon, this progress of accidie from the position of being a deadly sin, deserving of damnation, to the position first of a disease and finally of an essentially lyrical emotion, fruitful in the inspiration of much of the most characteristic modern literature. The sense of universal futility, the feelings of boredom and despair, with the complementary desire to be "anywhere, anywhere out of the world," or at least out of the place in which one happens at the moment to be, have been the inspiration of poetry and the novel for a century and more. It would have been inconceivable in Matthew Green's day to have written a serious poem about ennui. By Baudelaire's time ennui was as suitable a subject for lyric poetry as love; and accidie is still with us as an inspiration, one of the most serious and poignant of literary themes. What is the significance of this fact? For clearly the progress of accidie is a spiritual event of considerable importance. How is it to be explained?

It is not as though the nineteenth century invented accidie. Boredom, hopelessness and despair have always existed, and have been felt as poignantly in the past as we feel them now. Something has happened to make these emotions respectable and avowable; they are no longer sinful, no longer regarded as the mere symptoms of disease. That something that has happened is surely simply history since 1789. The failure of the French Revolution and the more spectacular downfall of Napoleon planted accidie in the heart of every youth of the Romantic generation—and not in France alone, but all over Europe—who believed in liberty or whose adolescence had been intoxicated by the ideas of glory and genius. Then came industrial progress with its prodigious multiplication of filth, misery and ill-gotten wealth; the defilement of nature by modern industry was in itself enough to sadden many sensitive minds. The discovery that political enfranchisement, so long and stubbornly fought for, was the merest futility and vanity so long as industrial servitude remained in force was another of the century's horrible disillusionments.

A more subtle cause of the prevalence of boredom was the disproportionate growth of the great towns. Habituated to the feverish existence of these few centres of activity, men found that life outside them was intolerably insipid. And at the same time they became so much exhausted by the restlessness of city life that they pined for the monotonous boredom of the provinces, for exotic islands, even for other worlds—any haven of rest. And finally, to crown this vast structure of failures and disillusionments, there came the appalling catastrophe of the War of 1914. Other epochs have witnessed disasters, have had to suffer disillusionment; but in no century have the disillusionments followed on one another's heels with such unintermitted rapidity as in the nineteenth and twentieth, for the good reason that in no centuries has change been so rapid and so profound. The *mal du siècle* was an inevitable evil; indeed, we can claim with a certain pride that we have a right to our accidie. With us it is not a sin or a disease of the hypochondries; it is a state of mind which fate has forced upon us.

BREUGHEL

MOST of our mistakes are fundamentally grammatical. We create our own difficulties by employing an inadequate language to describe facts. Thus, to take one example, we are constantly giving the same name to more than one thing, and more than one name to the same thing. The results, when we come to argue, are deplorable. For we are using a language which does not adequately describe the things about which we are arguing.

The word "painter" is one of those names whose indiscriminate application has led to the worst results. All those who, for whatever reason and with whatever intentions, put brushes to canvas and make pictures, are called without distinction, painters. Deceived by the uniqueness of the name, aestheticians have tried to make us believe that there is a single painter-psychology, a single function of painting, a single standard of criticism. Fashion changes and the views of art critics with it. At the present time it is fashionable to believe in form to the exclusion of subject. Young people almost swoon away with excess of aesthetic emo-

tion before a Matisse. Two generations ago
they would have been wiping their eyes before the latest Landseer. (Ah, those more
than human, those positively Christ-like dogs
—how they moved, what lessons they
taught! There had been no religious painting like Landseer's since Carlo Dolci died.)

These historical considerations should
make us chary of believing too exclusively in
any single theory of art. One kind of painting, one set of ideas are fashionable at any
given moment. They are made the basis
of a theory which condemns all other kinds
of painting and all preceding critical
theories. The process constantly repeats
itself.

At the present moment, it is true, we have
achieved an unprecedentedly tolerant eclecticism. We are able, if we are up-to-date,
to enjoy everything, from negro sculpture to
Luca della Robbia and from Magnasco to
Byzantine mosaics. But it is an eclecticism
achieved at the expense of almost the whole
content of the various works of art considered. What we have learned to see in all
these works is their formal qualities, which
we abstract and arbitrarily call essential.
The subject of the work, with all that the
painter desired to express in it beyond his
feelings about formal relations, contempo-

rary criticism rejects as unimportant. The young painter scrupulously avoids introducing into his pictures anything that might be mistaken for a story, or the expression of a view of life, while the young *Kunstforscher* turns, as though at an act of exhibitionism, from any manifestation by a contemporary of any such forbidden interest in drama or philosophy. True, the old masters are indulgently permitted to illustrate stories and express their thoughts about the world. Poor devils, they knew no better! Your modern observer makes allowance for their ignorance and passes over in silence all that is not a matter of formal relations. The admirers of Giotto (as numerous to-day as were the admirers of Guido Reni a hundred years ago) contrive to look at the master's frescoes without considering what they represent, or what the painter desired to express. Every germ of drama or meaning is disinfected out of them; only the composition is admired. The process is analogous to reading Latin verses without understanding them—simply for the sake of the rhythmical rumbling of the hexameters.

It would be absurd, of course, to deny the importance of formal relations. No picture can hold together without composition and no good painter is without some specific passion for form as such—just as no good writer is without a passion for words and the arrangement of words. It is obvious that no man can adequately express himself, unless he takes an interest in the terms which he proposes to use as his medium of expression. Not all painters are interested in the same sort of forms. Some, for example, have a passion for masses and the surfaces of solids. Others delight in lines. Some compose in three dimensions. Others like to make silhouettes on the flat. Some like to make the surface of the paint smooth and, as it were, translucent, so that the objects represented in the picture can be seen distinct and separate, as through a sheet of glass. Others (as for example Rembrandt) love to make a rich thick surface which shall absorb and draw together into one whole all the objects represented, and that in spite of the depth of the composition and the distance of the objects from the plane of the picture. All these purely aesthetic considerations are, as I have said, important. All artists are interested in them; but almost none are interested in them to the exclusion of everything else. It is very seldom indeed that we find a painter who can be inspired merely by his interest in form and texture to paint a picture. Good painters of "abstract" subjects or even

of still lives are rare.   Apples and solid geometry do not stimulate a man to express his
feelings about form and make a composition.
All thoughts and emotions are interdepend-
ent.   In the words of the dear old song,

> The roses round the door
> Make me love mother more.

One feeling is excited by another.   Our fac-
ulties work best in a congenial emotional
atmosphere.   For example, Mantegna's faculty for making noble arrangements of forms
was stimulated by his feelings about heroic
and god-like humanity.   Expressing those
feelings, which he found exciting, he also
expressed—and in the most perfect manner
of which he was capable—his feelings about
masses, surfaces, solids and voids.   "The
roses round the door"—his hero worship—
"made him love mother more"—made him,
by stimulating his faculty for composition,
paint better.   If Isabella d'Este had made
him paint apples, table napkins and bottles,
he would have produced, being uninterested
in these objects, a poor composition.   And
yet, from a purely formal point of view,
apples, bottles and napkins are quite as interesting as human bodies and faces.   But
Mantegna—and with him the majority of
painters—did not happen to be very pas-

sionately interested in these inanimate objects. When one is bored one becomes boring.

> The apples round the door
> Make me a frightful bore.

Inevitably, unless I happen to be so exclusively interested in form that I can paint anything that has a shape; or unless I happen to possess some measure of that queer pantheism, that animistic superstition which made Van Gogh regard the humblest of common objects as being divinely or devilishly alive. *"Crains dans le mur aveugle un regard qui t'épie."* If a painter can do that, he will be able, like Van Gogh, to make pictures of cabbage fields and the bedrooms of cheap hotels that shall be as wildly dramatic as a Rape of the Sabines.

The contemporary fashion is to admire beyond all others the painter who can concentrate on the formal side of his art and produce pictures which are entirely devoid of literature. Old Renoir's apophthegm, *"Un peintre, voyez-vous, qui a le sentiment du téton et des fesses, est un homme sauvé,"* is considered by the purists suspiciously latitudinarian. A painter who has the sentiment of the pap and the buttocks is a painter who portrays real models with gusto. Your pure aesthete should only have a feeling for hemispheres, curved lines and surfaces. But this "sentiment of the buttocks" is common to all good painters. It is the lowest common measure of the whole profession. It is possible, like Mantegna, to have a passionate feeling for all that is solid, and at the same time to be a stoic philosopher and a hero-worshipper; possible, with Michelangelo, to have a complete realization of breasts and also an interest in the soul or, like Rubens, to have a sentiment for human greatness as well as for human rumps. The greater includes the less; great dramatic or reflective painters know everything that the aestheticians who paint geometrical pictures, apples or buttocks know, and a great deal more besides. What they have to say about formal relations, though important, is only a part of what they have to express. The contemporary insistence on form to the exclusion of everything else is an absurdity. So was the older insistence on exact imitation and sentiment to the exclusion of form. There need be no exclusions. In spite of the single name, there are many different kinds of painters, and all of them, with the exception of those who cannot paint, and those whose minds are trivial, vulgar and tedious, have a right to exist.

All classifications and theories are made

after the event; the facts must first occur before they can be tabulated and methodized. Reversing the historical process, we attack the facts forearmed with theoretical prejudice. Instead of considering each fact on its own merits, we ask how it fits into the theoretical scheme. At any given moment a number of meritorious facts fail to fit into the fashionable theory and have to be ignored. Thus El Greco's art failed to conform with the ideal of good painting held by Philip the Second and his contemporaries. The Sienese primitives seemed to the seventeenth and eighteenth centuries incompetent barbarians. Under the influence of Ruskin, the later nineteenth century contrived to dislike almost all architecture that was not Gothic. And the early twentieth century, under the influence of the French, deplores and ignores, in painting, all that is literary, reflective or dramatic.

In every age theory has caused men to like much that was bad and reject much that was good. The only prejudice that the ideal art critic should have is against the incompetent, the mentally dishonest and the futile. The number of ways in which good pictures can be painted is quite incalculable, depending only on the variability of the human mind. Every good painter invents a new way of painting.   Is this man a competent painter? Has he something to say, is he genuine? These are the questions a critic must ask himself.   Not, Does he conform with my theory of imitation, or distortion, or moral purity, or significant form?

There is one painter against whom, it seems to me, theoretical prejudice has always most unfairly told.   I mean the elder Breughel. Looking at his best paintings I find that I can honestly answer in the affirmative all the questions which a critic may legitimately put himself.   He is highly competent aesthetically; he has plenty to say; his mind is curious, interesting and powerful; and he has no false pretensions, is entirely honest.   And yet he has never enjoyed the high reputation to which his merits entitle him.   This is due, I think, to the fact that his work has never quite squared with any of the various critical theories which since his days have had a vogue in the aesthetic world.

A subtle colourist, a sure and powerful draughtsman, and possessing powers of composition that enable him to marshal the innumerable figures with which his pictures are filled into pleasingly decorative groups (built up, as we see, when we try to analyze his methods of formal arrangement, out of individually flat, silhouette-like shapes standing

in a succession of receding planes), Breughel
can boast of purely aesthetic merits that ought
to endear him even to the strictest sect of the
Pharisees. Coated with this pure aesthetic
jam, the bitter pill of his literature might
easily, one would suppose, be swallowed. If
Giotto's dalliance with sacred history be forgiven him, why may not Breughel be excused
for being an anthropologist and a social philosopher? To which I tentatively answer:
Giotto is forgiven, because we have so utterly
ceased to believe in Catholic Christianity
that we can easily ignore the subject matter
of his pictures and concentrate only on their
formal qualities; Breughel, on the other
hand, is unforgivable because he made comments on humanity that are still interesting
to us. From his subject matter we cannot
escape; it touches us too closely to be ignored.
That is why Breughel is despised by all up-
to-date *Kunstforschers.*

And even in the past, when there was no
theoretical objection to the mingling of literature and painting, Breughel failed, for
another reason, to get his due. He was considered low, gross, a mere comedian, and as
such unworthy of serious consideration.
Thus, the *Encyclopaedia Britannica,* which
in these matters may be safely relied on to
give the current opinion of a couple of gen-

erations ago, informs us, in the eleven lines which it parsimoniously devotes to Peter Breughel, that "the subjects of his pictures are chiefly humorous figures, like those of D. Teniers; and if he wants the delicate touch and silvery clearness of that master, he has abundant spirit and comic power."

Whoever wrote these words—and they might have been written by any one desirous, fifty years ago, of playing for safety and saying the right thing—can never have taken the trouble to look at any of the pictures painted by Breughel when he was a grown and accomplished artist.

In his youth, it is true, he did a great deal of hack work for a dealer who specialized in caricatures and devils in the manner of Hieronymus Bosch. But his later pictures, painted when he had really mastered the secrets of his art, are not comic at all. They are studies of peasant life, they are allegories, they are religious pictures of the most strangely reflective cast, they are exquisitely poetical landscapes. Breughel died at the height of his powers. But there is enough of his mature work in existence—at Antwerp, at Brussels, at Naples, and above all at Vienna —to expose the fatuity of the classical verdict and exhibit him for what he was: the first landscape painter of his century, the acutest student of manners, and the wonderfully skilful pictorial expounder or suggester of a view of life. It is at Vienna, indeed, that Breughel's art can best be studied in all its aspects. For Vienna possesses practically all his best pictures of whatever kind. The scattered pictures at Antwerp, Brussels, Paris, Naples and elsewhere give one but the faintest notion of Breughel's powers. In the Vienna galleries are collected more than a dozen of his pictures, all belonging to his last and best period. The Tower of Babel, the great Calvary, the Numbering of the People at Bethlehem, the two Winter Landscapes and the Autumn Landscape, the Conversion of Saint Paul, the Battle between the Israelites and the Philistines, the Marriage Feast and the Peasant's Dance—all these admirable works are here. It is on these that he must be judged.

There are four landscapes at Vienna: the Dark Day (January) and Huntsmen in the Snow (February), a November landscape (the Return of the Cattle) and the Numbering of the People at Bethlehem, which in spite of its name is little more than a landscape with figures. This last, like the February Landscape and the Massacre of the Innocents at Brussels, is a study of snow. Snow scenes lent themselves particularly

well to Breughel's style of painting. For a
snowy background has the effect of making
all dark or coloured objects seen against it
appear in the form of very distinct, sharp-
edged silhouettes. Breughel does in all his
compositions what the snow does in nature.
All the objects in his pictures (which are
composed in a manner that reminds one very
much of the Japanese) are paper-thin silhouettes arranged, plane after plane, like the
theatrical scenery in the depth of the stage.
Consequently in the painting of snow scenes,
where nature starts by imitating his habitual
method, he achieves an almost disquieting
degree of fundamental realism. Those
hunters stepping down over the brow of the
hill towards the snowy valley with its frozen
ponds are Jack Frost himself and his crew.
The crowds who move about the white
streets of Bethlehem have their being in an
absolute winter, and those ferocious troopers
looting and innocent-hunting in the midst of
a Christmas card landscape are a part of the
very army of winter, and the innocents they
kill are the young green shoots of the earth.

Breughel's method is less fundamentally
compatible with the snowless landscapes of
January and November. The different
planes stand apart a little too flatly and distinctly. It needs a softer, bloomier kind of

painting to recapture the intimate quality of such scenes as those he portrays in these two pictures. A born painter of Autumn, for example, would have fused the beasts, the men, the trees and the distant mountains into a hazier unity, melting all together, the near and the far, in the rich surface of his paint. Breughel painted too transparently and too flatly to be the perfect interpreter of such landscapes. Still, even in terms of his not entirely suitable convention he has done marvels. The Autumn Day is a thing of the most exquisite beauty. Here, as in the more sombrely dramatic January Landscape, he makes a subtle use of golds and yellows and browns, creating a sober yet luminous harmony of colours. The November Landscape is entirely placid and serene; but in the Dark Day he has staged one of those natural dramas of the sky and earth—a conflict between light and darkness. Light breaks from under clouds along the horizon, shines up from the river in the valley that lies in the middle distance, glitters on the peaks of the mountains. The foreground, which represents the crest of a wooded hill, is dark; and the leafless trees growing on the slopes are black against the sky. These two pictures are the most beautiful sixteenth-century landscapes of which I have any knowledge. They are intensely poetical, yet sober and not excessively picturesque or romantic. Those fearful crags and beetling precipices of which the older painters were so fond do not appear in these examples of Breughel's maturest work.

Breughel's anthropology is as delightful as his nature poetry. He knew his Flemings, knew them intimately, both in their prosperity and during the miserable years of strife, of rebellion, of persecution, of war and consequent poverty which followed the advent of the Reformation in Flanders.

A Fleming himself, and so profoundly and ineradicably a Fleming that he was able to go to Italy, and, like his great countryman in the previous century, Roger van der Weyden, return without the faintest tincture of Italianism—he was perfectly qualified to be the natural historian of the Flemish folk. He exhibits them mostly in those moments of orgiastic gaiety with which they temper the laborious monotony of their daily lives: eating enormously, drinking, uncouthly dancing, indulging in that peculiarly Flemish scatological waggery. The Wedding Feast and the Peasants' Dance, both at Vienna, are superb examples of this anthropological type of painting. Nor must we forget those two curious pictures, the Battle between Car-

nival and Lent and the Children's Games.
They too show us certain aspects of the joyous side of Flemish life. But the view is
not of an individual scene, casually seized at
its height and reproduced. These two pictures are systematic and encyclopaedic. In
one he illustrates all children's games; in the
other all the amusements of carnival, with
all the forces arrayed on the side of asceticism. In the same way he represents, in his
extraordinary Tower of Babel, all the proc-
esses of building. These pictures are hand-
books of their respective subjects.

Breughel's fondness for generalizing and
systematizing is further illustrated in his allegorical pieces. The Triumph of Death, at
the Prado, is appalling in its elaboration and
completeness. The fantastic "Dulle Griet"
at Antwerp is an almost equally elaborate
triumph of evil. His illustrations to prov-
erbs and parables belong to the same class.
They show him to have been a man profoundly convinced of the reality of evil and
of the horrors which this mortal life, not to
mention eternity, hold in store for suffering
humanity. The world is a horrible place;
but in spite of this, or precisely because of
this, men and women eat, drink and dance,
Carnival tilts against Lent and triumphs, if
only for a moment; children play in the

streets, people get married in the midst of gross rejoicings.

But of all Breughel's pictures the one most richly suggestive of reflection is not specifically allegorical or systematic. Christ carrying the Cross is one of his largest canvases, thronged with small figures rhythmically grouped against a wide and romantic background. The composition is simple, pleasing in itself, and seems to spring out of the subject instead of being imposed on it. So much for pure aesthetics.

Of the Crucifixion and the Carrying of the Cross there are hundreds of representations by the most admirable and diverse masters. But of all that I have ever seen this Calvary of Breughel's is the most suggestive and, dramatically, the most appalling. For all other masters have painted these dreadful scenes from within, so to speak, outwards. For them Christ is the centre, the divine hero of the tragedy; this is the fact from which they start; it affects and transforms all the other facts, justifying, in a sense, the horror of the drama and ranging all that surrounds the central figure in an ordered hierarchy of good and evil. Breughel, on the other hand, starts from the outside and works inwards. He represents the scene as it would have appeared to any casual spectator on the road to Golgotha on a certain spring morning in the year A. D. 33. Other artists have pretended to be angels, painting the scene with a knowledge of its significance. But Breughel resolutely remains a human onlooker. What he shows is a crowd of people walking briskly in holiday joyfulness up the slopes of a hill. On the top of the hill, which is seen in the middle distance on the right, are two crosses with thieves fastened to them, and between them a little hole in the ground in which another cross is soon to be planted. Round the crosses, on the bare hill-top stands a ring of people, who have come out with their picnic baskets to look on at the free entertainment offered by the ministers of justice. Those who have already taken their stand round the crosses are the prudent ones; in these days we should see them with campstools and thermos flasks, six hours ahead of time, in the vanguard of the queue for a Melba night at Covent Garden. The less provident or more adventurous people are in the crowd coming up the hill with the third and greatest of the criminals whose cross is to take the place of honour between the other two. In their anxiety not to miss any of the fun on the way up, they forget that they will have to take back seats at the actual place of execution. But it may be, of course, that they have reserved their places, up there. At Tyburn one could get an excellent seat in a private box for half a crown; with the ticket in one's pocket, one could follow the cart all the way from the prison, arrive with the criminal and yet have a perfect view of the performance. In these later days, when cranky humanitarianism has so far triumphed that hangings take place in private and Mrs. Thompson's screams are not even allowed to be recorded on the radio, we have to be content with reading about executions, not with seeing them. The impresarios who sold seats at Tyburn have been replaced by titled newspaper proprietors who sell juicy descriptions of Tyburn to a prodigiously much larger public. If people were still hanged at Marble Arch, Lord Riddell would be much less rich.

That eager, tremulous, lascivious interest in blood and beastliness which in these more civilized days we can only satisfy at one remove from reality in the pages of our newspapers, was franklier indulged in Breughel's day; the naïve ingenuous brute in man was less sophisticated, was given longer rope, and joyously barks and wags its tail round the appointed victim. Seen thus, impassively, from the outside, the tragedy does not purge or uplift; it appals and makes desperate; or it may even inspire a kind of gruesome mirth. The same situation may often be either tragic or comic, according as it is seen through the eyes of those who suffer or those who look on. (Shift the point of vision a little and Macbeth could be paraphrased as a roaring farce.) Breughel makes a concession to the high tragic convention by placing in the foreground of his picture a little group made up of the holy women weeping and wringing their hands. They stand quite apart from the other figures in the picture and are fundamentally out of harmony with them, being painted in the style of Roger van der Weyden. A little oasis of passionate spirituality, an island of consciousness and comprehension in the midst of the pervading stupidity and brutishness. Why Breughel put them into his picture is difficult to guess; perhaps for the benefit of the conventionally religious, perhaps out of respect for tradition; or perhaps he found his own creation too depressing and added this noble irrelevance to reassure himself.

TIBET

IN moments of complete despair, when it seems that all is for the worst in the worst of all possible worlds, it is cheering to discover that there are places where stupidity reigns even more despotically than in Western Europe, where civilization is based on principles even more fantastically unreasonable. Recent experience has shown me that the depression into which the Peace, Mr. Churchill, the state of contemporary literature, have conspired to plunge the mind, can be sensibly relieved by a study, even superficial, of the manners and customs of Tibet. The spectacle of an ancient and elaborate civilization of which almost no detail is not entirely idiotic is in the highest degree comforting and refreshing. It fills us with hopes of the ultimate success of our own civilization; it restores our wavering self-satisfaction in being citizens of industrialized Europe. Compared with Tibet, we are prodigious. Let us cherish the comparison.

My informant about Tibetan civilization is a certain Japanese monk of the name of Kawaguchi, who spent three years in Tibet at the beginning of the present century. His account of the experience has been translated into English, and published, with the title *Three Years in Tibet*, by the Theosophical Society. It is one of the great travel books of the world, and, so far as I am aware, the most interesting book on Tibet that exists. Kawaguchi enjoyed opportunities in Tibet which no European traveller could possibly have had. He attended the University of Lhasa, he enjoyed the acquaintance of the Dalai Lama himself, he was intimate with one of the four Ministers of Finance, he was the friend of lama and layman, of all sorts and conditions of Tibetans, from the highest class to the lowest—the despicable caste of smiths and butchers. He knew his Tibet intimately; for those three years, indeed, he was for all practical purposes a Tibetan. This is something which no European explorer can claim, and it is this which gives Kawaguchi's book its unique interest.

The Japanese, like people of every other nationality except the Chinese, are not permitted to enter Tibet. Mr. Kawaguchi did not allow this to stand in the way of his pious mission—for his purpose in visiting Tibet was to investigate the Buddhist writings and traditions of the place. He made his way to India, and in a long stay at Darjeeling familiarized himself with the Tibetan

language. He then set out to walk across
the Himalayas. Not daring to affront the
strictly guarded gates which bar the direct
route to Lhasa, he penetrated Tibet at its
south-western corner, underwent prodigious
hardships in an uninhabited desert eighteen
thousand feet above sea-level, visited the
holy lake of Manosarovara, and finally, after
astonishing adventures, arrived in Lhasa.
Here he lived for nearly three years, passing
himself off as a Chinaman. At the end of
that time his secret leaked out, and he was
obliged to accelerate his departure for India.
So much for Kawaguchi himself, though I
should have liked to say more of him; for a
more charming and sympathetic character
never revealed himself in a book.

Tibet is so full of fantastic low comedy
that one hardly knows where to begin a catalogue of its absurdities. Shall we start with
the Tibetans' highly organized service of
trained nurses, whose sole duty it is to prevent
their patients from going to sleep? or with
the Dalai Lama's chief source of income—
the sale of pills made of dung, at, literally,
a guinea a box? or with the Tibetan custom
of never washing from the moment of birth,
when, however, they are plentifully anointed
with melted butter, to the moment of death?
And then there is the University of Lhasa,

which an eminent Cambridge philosopher has compared with the University of Oxford—somewhat unjustly perhaps; but let that pass. At the University of Lhasa the student is instructed in logic and philosophy; every year of his stay he has to learn by heart from one to five or six hundred pages of holy texts. He is also taught mathematics, but in Tibet this art is not carried farther than subtraction. It takes twenty years to get a degree at the University of Lhasa—twenty years, and then most of the candidates are ploughed. To obtain a superior Ph. D. degree, entitling one to become a really holy and eminent lama, forty years of application to study and to virtue are required. But it is useless to try to make a catalogue of the delights of Tibet. There are too many of them for mention in this small place. One can do no more than glance at a few of the brighter spots in the system.

There is much to be said for the Tibetan system of taxation. The Government requires a considerable revenue; for enormous sums have to be spent in keeping perpetually burning in the principal Buddhist cathedral of Lhasa an innumerable army of lamps, which may not be fed with anything cheaper than clarified yak butter. This is the heaviest item of expenditure. But a great deal of money also goes to supporting the Tibetan clergy, who must number at least a sixth of the total population. The money is raised by a poll tax, paid in kind, the amount of which, fixed by ancient tradition, may, theoretically, never be altered. Theoretically only; for the Tibetan Government employs in the collection of taxes no fewer than twenty different standards of weight and thirty-six different standards of measure. The pound may weigh anything from half to a pound and a half; and the same with the units of measure. It is thus possible to calculate with extraordinary nicety, according to the standard of weight and measure in which your tax is assessed, where precisely you stand in the Government's favour. If you are a notoriously bad character, or even if you are innocent, but live in a bad district, your tax will have to be paid in measures of the largest size. If you are virtuous, or, better, if you are rich, of good family and *bien pensant*, then you will pay by weights which are only half the nominal weight. For those whom the Government neither hates nor loves, but regards with more or less contempt or tolerance, there are the thirty-four intervening degrees.

Kawaguchi's final judgment of the Tibetans, after three years' intimate acquaintance with them, is not a flattering one:

"The Tibetans are characterized by four serious defects, these being: filthiness, superstition, unnatural customs (such as polyandry), and unnatural art. I should be sorely perplexed if I were asked to name their redeeming points; but if I had to do so, I should mention first of all the fine climate in the vicinity of Lhasa and Shigatze, their sonorous and refreshing voices in reading the Text, the animated style of their catechisms, and their ancient art."

Certainly a bad lot of vices; but then the Tibetan virtues are not lightly to be set aside. We English possess none of them: our climate is abominable, our method of reading the holy texts is painful in the extreme, our catechisms, at least in my young days, were far from animated, and our ancient art is very indifferent stuff. But still, in spite of these defects, in spite of Mr. Churchill and the state of contemporary literature, we can still look at the Tibetans and feel reassured.

BALLET IN CRITICISM:
CALLOT

THERE is no orchestra; but two-and-thirty players perform in unison upon as many harpsichords the most brilliant compositions of Domenico Scarlatti. The dry glitter of the instruments fills and exhilarates the air. It is a music that might cure phthisis.

The scene represents a flat and almost limitless plain, quite bare except for a few small Italian houses, miles away on the horizon, and a vast oak tree which rises a little to the right of the centre and within a few feet of the back of the stage. There are no leaves on the tree. It is winter, and the grey, intense light of a northern day illumines the scene.

In the foreground and to the left, a company of vagabond actors are grouped around their hooded waggon. Here are Guarsetto and Mestolino in their linen coats and baggy trousers, their shovel hats stuck with parrots' feathers, their goat's beards and paper noses. Razullo in tights, tattered jerkin and page's cap, plays on a guitar, whose little belly and interminable long neck make it the very antithesis of Curcurucu, who carries— cautiously, carefully, tremulously on a poor, thin pair of legs—a great paunch, hunched shoulders, and a jutting rump. Fracischina and Signora Lucia are dressed in long, flowing skirts, tight bodice, sleeves like a bishop's, fluttering ringlets.

Opposite, on the right of the stage, a group of ladies and gentlemen, gipsies, beggars, idiots, stand watching them. In the open space between, the actors step out and dance.

They dance, alone, in pairs and trios, in every variety of combination. Now it is Franca Trippa and Fritellino kicking up their heels at one another in a sly, low jig. Now Signora Lucia steps nobly and gracefully through a pavane, while Razullo postures over his guitar, showing off the elegance of his legs in a series of lunging steps. Curcurucu walks behind him, trying to imitate, as well as his belly and his feeble legs will allow, these heroical attitudes. They are followed by Fracischina and the two satyr-pantaloons. They dance as though intoxicated; not with wine or any of the grosser joys, but with some more rarefied poison. They dance as though they were philosophers who had succeeded at last in picking the lock of the Absolute's back door. They dance as though they had discovered in a sudden flash that life is what it is. The pantaloons dance with their arms akimbo, their hands twisted back downwards, jutted rump answering to jutted belly—a bounding hornpipe. Arms upstretched and beating a tambourine above her head, Fracischina is all aspiring lines and vertical leaping. She is the living, leaping maypole, and the pantaloons, Guarsetto and Mestolino, go leaping round her. They dance, they dance as though they would never stop.

In the midst of their dancing, across the dry and glittering music of the harpsichords is heard, far off, the disquieting sound of drums, beating a march. It grows louder and louder, till at last, at the back of the stage, there files in a company of pikemen. Behind the dancing philosophers the soldiers manœuvre. Their long pikes come together, fall apart, making arithmetical patterns against the sky. It is a grave Pythagorean dance of pure Number.

When, panting, Fracischina and the pantaloons have made an end, the leaders of this troop, redoubtable Captain Malagamba, redoubtable Buonavita, dressed, like all the other gentlemen, in the romantic uniform of Puss-in-Boots, come striding forward. Theirs is a stamping dance of swashbucklers.

The pikes continue to manœuvre against the colourless sky.

A scene of descriptive pantomime follows the dance. The Captains point up towards the branches of the oak tree; then, turning to their pikemen, make a signal of command. The ranks divide; we see a pinioned prisoner kneeling at the feet of a friar, who holds aloft a crucifix and with choreographic gestures exhorts to repentance. The ranks close again.

It is a little matter of hanging.

The company applauds: "Bravissimo!" Then in a ring, actors, idiots, gentry, beggars and gipsies—all hand in hand—dance round the two Captains, who blow kisses and bow their appreciation of the compliment.

The ring breaks up. Six acrobats enter with a long ladder and a rope. They balance the ladder on end, climb up, slide down. All the tricks that one can do with a ladder are done. It is set up at last against the tree, and the rope is fastened to the principal branch so that the noose hangs at a point immediately above the centre of the stage.

The ranks reopen. Slowly the prisoner and the gesticulating friar advance. All crowd forward, turning their backs on the audience, to witness the spectacle. Captain Malagamba takes the opportunity to embrace the Signora Lucia. She, at the imminence of his amorous whiskers, starts away from him. Malagamba follows; there is a brief dance of retreat and pursuit. The Captain has driven her into a corner, between the shafts of the waggon, and is about to ravish an embracement in good earnest, when Razullo, happening to look round, sees what is going on. Brandishing his long-necked guitar, he bounds across the stage, and with one magistral blow lays out the Captain along the floor. Then, pirouetting, he slips off with the delivered Signora. Meanwhile, the prisoner has been led forward to the foot of the ladder, on the rungs of which, like a troop of long-limbed monkeys, gambol the playful acrobats. The spectators have eyes for nothing else.

One of the village idiots, who lacks the wit to appreciate the charms of the spectacle, sees as he gapes vacantly about him the prostrate carcase of Malagamba, approaches, and bends over it in imbecile sympathy. Malagamba utters a groan; some one in the crowd looks round, calls the attention of the rest. There is a rush. The imbecile is seized, Malagamba raised to his feet, plied with strong waters from a bottle. Buonavita interrogates the idiot, who is held, smiling and drivelling, between two arquebusiers.

While, in the foreground, the descriptive pantomime of the idiot's examination, trial and condemnation is being danced through, behind and above the heads of the spectators, the acrobats are hauling the prisoner up the ladder; they have slipped the noose over his head, they have turned him off. His feet dance a double-shuffle on the wind, then gradually are still.

Captain Buonavita has by this time duly sentenced the idiot to execution. Still smiling, he is led down stage towards the foot of the ladder. The friar proffers him the crucifix.

Everybody dances. Malagamba has by this time sufficiently recovered to seize the vaulting Fracischina by the waist and toss her up into the air. The beggars, the Puss-in-Boots gentlemen, the actors, the idiots even—each seizes a partner, throws her up, brings her floating slowly down, as though reluctant to come to earth again. Fritellino and Franca Trippa jig in and out among the couples, slapping at them with their wooden swords. And the two pantaloons, who know that the world is what it is and are intoxicated with a truth that is 43 per cent above proof, go leaping and leaping, back and forth, across the front of the stage.

Still smiling, the idiot is coaxed up the

rungs of the ladder.   Like the debonairest
of black spider-monkeys, the acrobats frisk
around him, and in the extreme background
the moving pikes come together, break apart,
asserting unanswerably that two and two
make four and that five over blue beans is
the number of blue beans that make five.

As the spider-monkeys drop the noose over
the idiot's head there is a long commanding
roll of drums.   All turn round towards the
ladder, forming up in an ordered line across
the stage; they stand quite still.   Only the
two pantaloons, intent on their hornpipe,
dance on to the glittering phrases of the
harpsichords.

The drums roll on.   The noose is tight-
ened.   For the last time the friar raises his
crucifix towards the idiot's lips; the idiot
roars with laughter.   The drums change
their rhythm to the rub-a-dub rataplan of a
dancing march.   Without changing their
positions the spectators begin to mark time,
heel and toe.   Their feet twinkle, their heads
bob up and down.   The spider-monkeys
make a sudden gesture, and the idiot is
turned off to swing by the side of the other
victim.   His feet as they tread air keep time
with the drums and the silent heel and toe
of those who beat the solid earth.   Rub-a-
dub rataplan, rataplan, rub-dub.

Suddenly there is silence; drums and harpsichords are still. From far off there comes a sound of singing; it swells, it increases, piercingly beautiful. A procession of monks and choristers passes slowly across the stage. They are singing the Tenebrae of Vittoria. *Dum crucifixissent Jesum. . . .* The voices rise and fall, cross and interpenetrate—five solitary agonies that have come together to make a final sixth and more appalling, a sixth and more piercing, more beautiful agony. Slowly the priests and choristers cross the stage; the music swells and then once more decreases, fading, fainting along the air.

The Puss-in-Boots Captains and the gentlemen, the actors, the beggars, the gipsies and the idiots stare after the retreating procession in an open-mouthed astonishment. And well they may, for the impresario has made an absurd mistake. This music belongs to an entirely different ballet.

MODERN FOLK POETRY

TO all those who are interested in the "folk" and their poetry—the contemporary folk of the great cities and their urban muse—I would recommend a little-known journal called *McGlennon's Pantomime Annual*. This periodical makes its appearance at some time in the New Year, when the pantos are slowly withering away under the influence of approaching spring. I take this opportunity of warning my readers to keep a sharp look-out for the coming of the next issue; it is sure to be worth the modest two-pence which one is asked to pay for it.

McGlennon's Pantomime Annual is an anthology of the lyrics of the panto season's most popular songs. It is a document of first-class importance. To the future student of our popular literature *McGlennon* will be as precious as the Christie-Miller collection of Elizabethan broadsheets. In the year 2220 a copy of the *Pantomime Annual* may very likely sell for hundreds of pounds at the Sotheby's of the time. With laudable forethought I am preserving my copy of last year's *McGlennon* for the enrichment of my distant posterity.

The Folk Poetry of 1920 may best be classified according to subject matter. First, by reason of its tender associations as well as its mere amount, is the Poetry of Passion. Then there is the Poetry of Filial Devotion. Next, the Poetry of the Home—the dear old earthly Home in Oregon or Kentucky—and, complementary to it, the Poetry of the Spiritual Home in other and happier worlds. Here, as well as in the next section, the popular lyric borrows some of its best effects from hymnology. There follows the Poetry of Recollection and Regret, and the Poetry of Nationality, a type devoted almost exclusively to the praises of Ireland. These types and their variations cover the Folk's serious poetry. Their comic vein is less susceptible to analysis. Drink, Wives, Young Nuts, Honeymoon Couples—these are a few of the stock subjects.

The Amorous Poetry of the Folk, like the love lyrics of more cultured poets, is divided into two species: the Poetry of Spiritual Amour and the more direct and concrete expression of Immediate Desire. *McGlennon* provides plenty of examples of both types:

When love peeps in the window of your heart

[it might be the first line of a Shakespeare sonnet]

You seem to walk on air,
Birds sing their sweet songs to you,
No cloud in your skies of blue,
Sunshine all the happy day, etc.

These rhapsodies tend to become a little tedious. But one feels the warm touch of reality in

I want to snuggle, I want to snuggle,
I know a cozy place for two.
I want to snuggle, I want to snuggle,
I want to feel that love is true.

Take me in your arms as lovers do,
Hold me very tight and kiss me too.
I want to snuggle, I want to snuggle,
I want to snuggle close to you.

This is sound; but it does not come up to the best of the popular lyrics. The agonized passion expressed in the words and music of "You Made Me Love You" is something one does not easily forget, though that great song is as old as the now distant origins of ragtime.

The Poetry of Filial Devotion is almost as extensive as the Poetry of Amour. *McGlennon* teems with such outbursts as this:

You are a wonderful mother, dear old mother of
    mine.
You'll hold a spot down deep in my heart
Till the stars no longer shine.

> Your soul shall live on for ever,
> On through the fields of time,
> For there'll never be another to me
> Like that wonderful mother of mine.

Even Grandmamma gets a share of this devotion:

> Granny, my own, I seem to hear you calling me;
> Granny, my own, you are my sweetest memory . . .
> If up in heaven angels reign supreme,
> Among the angels you must be the Queen.
> Granny, my own, I miss you more and more.

The last lines are particularly rich. What a fascinating heresy, to hold that the angels reign over their Creator!

The Poetry of Recollection and Regret owes most, both in words and music, to the hymn. *McGlennon* provides a choice example in "Back from the Land of Yesterday":

> Back from the land of yesterday,
>   Back to the friends of yore;
> Back through the dark and dreary way
>   Into the light once more.
> Back to the heart that waits for me
>   Warmed by the sunshine above;
> Back from the old land of yesterday's dreams
>   To a new land of life and love.

What it means, goodness only knows. But one can imagine that, sung to a slow music in three-four time—some rich religious waltz-tune—it would be extremely uplifting and edifying. The decay of regular church-going has inevitably led to this invasion of the music-hall by the hymn. People still want to feel the good uplifting emotion, and they feel it with a vengeance when they listen to songs about

> the land of beginning again,
> Where skies are always blue . . .
> Where broken dreams come true.

The great advantage of the music-hall over the church is that the uplifting moments do not last too long.

Finally, there is the great Home motif. "I want to be," these lyrics always begin, "I want to be almost anywhere that is not the place where I happen at the moment to be." M. Louis Estève has called this longing "Le Mal de la Province," which in its turn is closely related to "Le Mal de l'au-delà." It is one of the worst symptoms of romanticism.

> Steamer, balançant ta mâture,
> Lève l'ancre vers une exotique nature,

exclaims Mallarmé, and the Folk, whom that most exquisite of poets loathed and despised, echo his words in a hundred different keys. There is not a State in America where they don't want to go. In *McGlennon* we find yearnings expressed for California, Ohio, Tennessee, Virginia, and Georgia. Some sigh for Ireland, Devon, and the East. "Egypt! I am calling you; Oh, life is sweet and joys complete when at your feet I lay [*sic*]." But the Southern States, the East, Devon, and Killarney are not enough. The Mal de l'au-delà succeeds the Mal de la Province. The Folk yearn for extra-mundane worlds. Here, for example, is an expression of nostalgia for a mystical "Kingdom within your eyes":

> Somewhere in somebody's eyes
> Is a place just divine,
> Bounded by roses that kiss the dew
> In those dear eyes that shine.
>
> Somewhere beyond earthly dreams,
> Where love's flower never dies,
> God made the world, and He gave it to me
> In that kingdom within your eyes.

If there is any characteristic which distinguishes contemporary folk poetry from the folk poetry of other times it is surely its meaninglessness. Old folk poetry is singularly direct and to the point, full of pregnant meaning, never vague. Modern folk poetry, as exemplified in *McGlennon*, is almost perfectly senseless. The Elizabethan peasant or mechanic would never have consented to sing or listen to anything so flatulently mean-

ingless as "Back from the Land of Yesterday" or "The Kingdom within your eyes."
His taste was for something clear, definite
and pregnant, like "Greensleeves":

> And every morning when you rose,
> I brought you dainties orderly,
> To clear your stomach from all woes—
> And yet you would not love me.

Could anything be more logical and to the
point? But we, instead of logic, instead of
clarity, are provided by our professional en-
tertainers with the drivelling imbecility of
"Granny, my own." Can it be that the
standard of intelligence is lower now than
it was three hundred years ago? Have newspapers and cinemas and now the wireless
telephone conspired to rob mankind of whatever sense of reality, whatever power of individual questioning and criticism he once possessed? I do not venture to answer. But
the fact of *McGlennon* has somehow got to
be explained. How? I prefer to leave the
problem on a note of interrogation.

RIMINI AND ALBERTI

RIMINI was honoured, that morning, by the presence of three distinguished visitors—ourselves and the Thaumaturgical Arm of St. Francis Xavier. Divorced from the rest of the saint's remains, whose home is a jewelled tabernacle in the church of Jesus at Old Goa, the Arm, like ourselves, was making an Italian tour. But while we poor common tourists were spending money on the way, the Thaumaturgical Arm—and this was perhaps its most miraculous achievement—was raking it in. It had only to show itself through the crystal window of the reliquary in which it travelled—a skeleton arm, with a huge amethyst ring still glittering on one of the fingers of its bony hand— to command the veneration of all beholders and a copper collection, thinly interspersed with nickel and the smallest paper. The copper collection went to the foreign missions: what happened to the veneration, I do not venture to guess. It was set down, no doubt, with their offered pence, to the credit of those who felt it, in the recording angel's book.

I felt rather sorry for St. Francis Xavier's

arm. The body of the saint, after translation from China to Malacca and from Malacca to India, now reposes, as I have said, in
the gaudy shrine at Goa. After a life so extraordinarily strenuous as was his, the great
missionary deserves to rest in peace. And
so he does, most of him. But his right arm
has had to forgo its secular quiet; its missionary voyages are not yet over. In its gold
and crystal box it travels indefatigably
through Catholic Christendom collecting
pence—"for spoiling Indian innocence," as
Mr. Matthew Green tersely and rather tartly
put it, two hundred years ago. Poor Arm!

We found it, that morning, in the church
of San Francesco at Rimini. A crowd of
adorers filled the building and overflowed
into the street outside. The people seemed
to be waiting rather vaguely in the hope
of something thaumaturgical happening.
Within the church, a long queue of men and
women shuffled slowly up into the choir to
kiss the jewelled bone-box and deposit their
soldi. Outside, among the crowd at the door
of the church, stood a number of hawkers,
selling picture post cards of the Thaumaturgical Arm and brief but fabulous biog-
raphies of its owner. We got into conversation with one of them, who told us that he
followed the Arm from town to town, selling

his wares wherever it stopped to show itself. The business seemed a tolerably profitable one; it enabled him, at any rate, to keep a wife and family living in comfort at Milan. He showed us their photographs; mother and children—they all looked well nourished. But, poor fellow! his business kept him almost uninterruptedly away from home. "What does one marry for?" he said as he put the photographs back into his pocket. "What?" He sighed and shook his head. If only the Arm could be induced to settle down for a little!

During the lunch hour the Arm was taken for a drive round Rimini. Red and yellow counterpanes were hung out of all the windows in its honour; the faithful waited impatiently. And at last it came, driving in a very large, very noisy and dirty old Fiat, accompanied, not, as one might have expected, by the ecclesiastical dignitaries of the city, but by seven or eight very secular young men in black shirts, with frizzy hair, their trouser pockets bulging with automatic pistols—the committee of the local Fascio, no doubt.

The Arm occupied the front seat, next the driver: the Fascists lolled behind. As the car passed, the faithful did a very curious thing; mingling the gestures of reverence and applause, they fell on their knees and clapped their hands. The Arm was treated as though it were a combination of Jackie Coogan and the Host. After lunch, it was driven rapidly away to Bologna. The vendors of sacred pictures followed as fast as the Italian trains would take them, the crowd dispersed, and the church of San Francesco reverted to its habitual silence.

For this we were rather glad; for it was not to see a fragment of St. Francis Xavier that we had come to Rimini; it was to look at the church of St. Francis of Assisi. Sight-seeing, so long as the Arm was there, had been impossible; its departure left us free to look round at our ease. Still, I was very glad that we had seen the peripatetic relic and its adorers in San Francesco. In this strange church which Malatesta found a Christian temple, rebuilt in pagan form and rededicated to himself, his mistress and the humanities, the scenes we had just witnessed possessed a certain piercing incongruousness that provoked—the wit of circumstances—a kind of meditative mirth. I tried to imagine what the first St. Francis would have thought of Sigismondo Malatesta, what Sigismondo thought of him, and how he would have regarded the desecration of his Nietzschean temple by this posthumous visit of a bit of the second St. Francis. One can imagine a pleasant little Gobinesque or Lucianic dialogue between the four of them in the Elysian Fields, a light and airy skating over the most fearful depths of the spirit. And for those who have ears to hear there is eloquence in the dumb disputation of the stones. The Gothic arches of the interior protest against the Roman shell with which Alberti enclosed St. Francis's church; protest against Matteo de'Pasti's pagan decorations and Malatesta's blasphemous self-exaltation; protest, while they commend the missionary's untiring disinterestedness, against the excessive richness of his Jesuit reliquary. Grave, restrained and intellectual, Alberti's classical façade seems to deplore the *naïveté* of the first St. Francis and the intolerant enthusiasms of the second, and, praising Malatesta's intelligence, to rebuke him for his lusts and excesses. Malatesta, meanwhile, laughs cynically at all of them. Power, pleasure and Isotta—these, he announces, through the scheme of decorations which he made Matteo de'Pasti carry out, these are the only things that matter.

The exterior of the church is entirely Alberti's. Neither St. Francis nor Malatesta are allowed to disturb its solemn and harmonious beauty. Its façade is a triumphal arch, a nobler version of that arch of Augustus which spans the street at the other end of Rimini.   In the colossal thickness of the southern wall, Alberti has pierced a series of deep arched niches.   Recessed shadow alternates harmoniously down a long perspective with smooth sunlit stone; and in every niche, plain and severe like the character of an early Roman in the pages of Plutarch, stands the sarcophagus of a scholar or a philosopher. There is nothing here of St. Francis's prelapsarian ingenuousness.   Alberti is an entirely conscious adult; he worships, but worships reason, rationally.   The whole building is a hymn to intellectual beauty, an exaltation of reason as the only source of human greatness.   Its form is Roman; for Rome was the retrospective Utopia in which such men as Alberti, from the time of the Renaissance down to a much later date, saw the fulfilment of their ideals.   The Roman myth dies hard, the Greek harder still; there are certain victims of a classical education who still regard the Republic as the home of all virtues and see in Periclean Athens the unique repository of human intelligence.

Malatesta would have got a better personal apotheosis if he had lived in a later century.   Alberti was too severe and stoical

an artist to condescend to mere theatrical
grandiosity. Nor, indeed, was the art of
being grandiose really understood till the
seventeenth century, the age of baroque, of
kingly and clerical display. The hard-work-
ing missionary, whose arm we had seen that
morning in Malatesta's temple, reposes at
Goa in the sort of surroundings that would
be perfectly suitable in a tyrant's self-raised
shrine. Alberti's monument, on the contrary, is a tribute to intellectual greatness.
As a memorial to a particularly cunning and
murderous ruffian it is absurd.

In the interior of the church, it is true,
Malatesta had things all his own way. Alberti was not there to interfere in his scheme
of decoration, so that Sigismondo was able
to dictate to Matteo de' Pasti and his col-
leagues all the themes of their carving. The
interior is consequently one vast personal
tribute to Malatesta and Isotta, with an occasional good word in favour of the pagan
gods, of literature, art and science. The too
expressive theatrical gesture of the baroque
architects and decorators had not yet been invented; Sigismondo's vulgar tyranny is consequently celebrated in the most perfect taste
and in terms of a delicate and learned fantasy. Sigismondo got better than his deserts;
he deserved Borromini, the Cavaliere Arpino

and a tenth-rate imitator of Bernini. What he actually got, owing to the accident of his date, was Matteo de' Pasti, Piero della Francesca and Leon Battista Alberti.

Alberti's share in the monument, then, is a kind of hymn to intellectual beauty, a paean in praise of civilization couched in the language of Rome—but freely and not pedantically employed, as the philosophers and the poets of the age employed the Latin idiom. To my mind, he was almost the noblest Roman of them all. The exterior of San Francesco at Rimini, the interior of Sant' Andrea at Mantua (sadly daubed about by later decorators and with Juvara's absurd high-drummed cupola in the midst instead of the saucer dome designed by Alberti himself), are as fine as anything in the whole range of Renaissance architecture. What renders them the more remarkable is that they were without precedent in his age. Alberti was one of the re-inventors of the style. Of his particular Roman manner, indeed (the manner which became the current idiom of the later Renaissance), he was the sole rediscoverer. The other early Renaissance manner, based, like Alberti's on the classics— the manner of Brunelleschi—was doomed, so far at any rate as ecclesiastical architecture was concerned, to extinction. Sant' Andrea at Mantua is the model from which the typical churches of the later Renaissance were imitated, not Brunelleschi's Florentine San Lorenzo or Santo Spirito.

A comparison between these nearly contemporary architects—Brunelleschi was born some twenty-five years before Alberti—is extremely interesting and instructive. Both were enthusiastic students of the antique, both knew their Rome, both employed in their buildings the characteristic elements of classical architecture. And yet it would be difficult to discover two architects whose work is more completely dissimilar. Compare the interiors of Brunelleschi's two Florentine churches with that of Alberti's Sant' Andrea. Brunelleschi's churches are divided into a nave and aisles by rows of tall slender pillars supporting round arches. The details are classical and so correct that they might have been executed by Roman workmen. But the general design is not Roman, but Romanesque. His churches are simply more spidery versions of eleventh-century basilicas, with "purer" details. All is airiness and lightness; there is even a certain air of insecurity about these church interiors, so slender are the pillars, so much free space is to be seen.

What a contrast with Alberti's great

church! It is built in the form of a Latin cross, with a single nave and side chapels. The nave is barrel-vaulted; over the crossing is a dome (Juvara's, unfortunately, not Alberti's); the altar is placed in an apse. The chapels open on to the central nave by tall, and proportionately wide, round-headed arches. Between each of the chapels is a gigantic pier of masonry, as wide as the arches which they separate. A small door is pierced in each of these piers, giving access to subsidiary chapels hollowed out of their mass. But the doors are inconspicuous, and the general effect is one of void and solid equally alternating. Alberti's is essentially the architecture of masses, Brunelleschi's of lines. Even to the enormous dome of Santa Maria del Fiore, Brunelleschi contrives to impart an extraordinary lightness, as of lines with voids between them. The huge mass hangs aerially from its eight ribs of marble. A miracle is effortlessly consummated before our eyes. But a dome, however light you make it, is essentially an affair of masses. In designing his cupola for Santa Maria del Fiore, Brunelleschi found the plastic view of things imposed upon him. That is why, it may be, the dome is so incomparably the finest thing he ever made. He was not permitted by the nature of the architectural problem to be solved to give free play to his passion for lightness and the fine line. He was dealing here with masses; it could not be escaped. The result was that, treating the mass of the dome as far as was possible in terms of light, strong, leaping lines, he contrived to impart to his work an elegance and an aerial strength such as have never been equalled in any other dome. The rest of Brunelleschi's work, however charming and graceful, is, to my mind at any rate, far less satisfying, precisely because it is so definitely an affair of lines. Brunelleschi studied the architecture of the Romans; but he took from it only its details. What was essential in it—its majestic massiveness—did not appeal to him. He preferred, in all his church designs, to refine and refine on the work of the Romanesque architects, until at last he arrived at a slender and precarious elegance that was all vacuum and outline.

Alberti, on the other hand, took from the Romans their fundamental conception of an architecture of masses and developed it, with refinements, for modern Christian uses. To my mind, he was the better and truer architect of the two. For I personally like massiveness and an air of solidity. Others, I know, prefer lines and lightness and would put the interior of San Lorenzo above that

of Sant' Andrea, the Pazzi chapel above
San Francesco at Rimini. We shall never
be reconciled. All who practise the visual
arts and, presumably, all who appreciate
them must have some kind of feeling for
form as such. But not all are interested in
the same kind of forms. The lovers of pure
line and the lovers of mass stand at opposite
ends of an aesthetic scale. The aesthetic passion of one artist, or one art lover, is solidity;
another is moved only by linear arabesques
on a flat surface. Those formal passions
may be misplaced. Painters may be led by
their excessive love of three-dimensional
solidity quite beyond the field of painting;
Michelangelo is an obvious example. Sculptors with too great a fondness for mere linear
effect cease to be sculptors, and their work is
no more than a flat decoration in stone or
metal, meant to be seen from only one point
of view and having no depth; the famous
Diana attributed to Goujon (but probably
by Benvenuto Cellini) is one of these statues
conceived in the flat. Just as painters must
not be too fond of solidity, nor sculptors too
much attached to flatness, so, it seems to me,
no architect should be too exclusively interested in lines. Architecture in the hands of
a linear enthusiast takes on the too slender,
spidery elegance of Brunelleschi's work.

The psycho-analysts, who trace all interest in art back to an infantile love of excrement, would doubtless offer some simple faecal explanation for the varieties in our aesthetic passions. One man loves masses, another lines: the explanation in terms of coprophily is so obvious that I may be excused from giving it here. I will content myself by quoting from the works of Dr. Ernest Jones the reason why the worship of form should come to be connected in so many cases with the worship of a moral ideal; in a word, why art is so often religious. "Religion," says Dr. Jones, "has always used art in one form or another, and must do so, for the reason that incestuous desires invariably construct their phantasies out of the material provided by the unconscious memory of infantile coprophilic interests; that is the inner meaning of the phrase, 'Art is the handmaid of Religion.'" Illuminating and beautiful words! It is a pity they were not written thirty years ago. I should have liked to read Tolstoy's comments in *What is Art?* on this last and best of the aesthetic theories.

CRÉBILLON THE YOUNGER

PROPHECY is mainly interesting for the light it throws on the age in which it is uttered. The Apocalypse, for example, tells us how a Christian felt about the world at the end of the first century. Manifestly ludicrous as a forecast, Mercier's *L' An 2240* is worth reading, because it shows us what were the ideals of an earnest and rather stupid Frenchman in the year 1770. And the ideals of an earnest and very intelligent Englishman of the early twentieth century may be studied, in all their process of development, in the long series of Mr. Wells's prophetic books. Our notions of the future have something of that significance which Freud attributes to our dreams. And not our notions of the future only: our notions of the past as well. For if prophecy is an expression of our contemporary fears and wishes, so too, to a very great extent, is history—or at least what passes for history among the mass of ordinary unprofessional folk. Utopias, earthly paradises and earthly hells are flowers of the imagination which contrive to blossom and luxuriate even in the midst of the stoniest dates and documents, even within the fixed and narrow boundaries of established fact. The works of St. Thomas survive; we have a record of the acts of Innocent III. But that does not prevent our pictures of the Middle Ages from being as various and as highly coloured as our pictures of Utopia, the Servile State or the New Jerusalem. We see the past through the refractive medium of our prejudices, our tastes, our contemporary fears and hopes. The facts of history exist; but they hardly trouble us. We select and interpret our documents till they square with our theories.

The eighteenth century is a period which has been interpreted and re-interpreted in the most surprisingly various ways: by its own philosophers (for the eighteenth century was highly self-conscious) as the age of reason and enlightenment; by the Romantics and their strange heirs, the Reactionaries and the Early Victorians, as the age of vice and spiritual drought; by the later nineteenth-century sceptics, who curiously combined the strictest Protestant morality with the most dogmatically anti-Christian philosophy, as an age of reason indeed, but of more than dubious character; by the Beardsleyites of the 'nineties, as an epoch of deliciously depraved frivolity, of futile and therefore truly aesthetic elegance. The popular conception of the eighteenth century at the present day is a mixture of Beardsley's and Voltaire's. We find its morals and its manners in the highest degree "amusing"; and when we want a stick to beat the corpses of the Eminent Victorians we apply to Hume or Gibson, to Voltaire or Helvétius, to Horace Walpole or Madame du Deffand. For the simpler-minded among us, the eighteenth century is summed up by Mr. Nigel Playfair's version of *The Beggar's Opera*. The more sophisticated find their *dix-huitième* in the original French documents (judiciously selected) or in the ironic pages of Mr. Lytton Strachey.

Charming historical Utopia! A moment's thought, however, is sufficient to show how arbitrarily we have abstracted it from reality. For who, after all, were the most important, the most durable and influential men that the century produced? The names of Bach, Handel and Mozart present themselves immediately to the mind; of Swedenborg and Wesley and Blake; of Dr. Johnson, Bishop Berkeley and Kant. Of none of these can it be said that he fits very easily into the scheme of *The Beggar's Opera*. True, our pianists and conductors have tried, Procrustes-like, to squeeze the musicians into

the *dix-huitième* mould. They play Bach
mechanically, Handel lightly, Mozart friv-
olously, without feeling and therefore without sense, and call the process a "classical"
interpretation. But let that pass. The fact
remains that the greatest men of the eighteenth century are not in the least what we
should call *dix-huitième*.

It must not be imagined, however, that our
particular "eighteenth century" is completely mythical. Something like it did genuinely exist, during a couple of generations,
among a small class of people in most European countries, especially France. The fact
that we have chosen to recreate a whole historical epoch in the image of this intel-
lectually free and morally licentious *dix-
huitième* throws some light on our own problems, our own twentieth-century bugbears,
our own desires. For a certain section of
contemporary society the terms "modern"
and "eighteenth century" are almost synonymous. Like our ancestors, we too are in revolt against intellectual authority and moral
"prejudices." Perhaps the chief difference
between them and us is that they believed
in pure reason as well as extra-conjugal love;
we Bergsonians do not.

One of the most characteristic representa-
tives of this particular *dix-huitième* which

we have chosen to exalt at the expense of all
the other possible eighteenth centuries is
Crébillon the Younger. We find in his
novels all the qualities which we regard as
typical of the period: elegance, frivolity, a
complete absence of moral "prejudices,"
especially on the subject of love, a certain
dry spirit of detachment and analysis. *Le
Sopha* and *La Nuit et le Moment* are documents which, taken by themselves, completely justify our current conception of the
age in which they were written. For that reason alone they deserve to be read. One should
always be prepared to quote authorities in
support of one's theories. Moreover, they
are worth reading for their own sakes. For
Crébillon was a psychologist and, in his own
limited field, one of the most acute of his
age.

The typically modern method of presenting character differs from that employed by
the novelists of the eighteenth century. In
our novels we offer the facts in a so-to-speak
raw state, leaving the reader to draw his own
conclusions from them. The older psychologists treated the facts to a preliminary
process of intellectual digestion; they gave
their readers something more than the mere
behaviouristic material on which psychological judgments are based; they gave them the

conclusions they themselves had already
drawn from the facts. Compare Constant's
Adolphe with the *Ulysses* of James Joyce;
the difference of method is manifest. Crébillon is a characteristic eighteenth-century
psychologist. With the dry intellectual precision of his age, he describes and comments
on his characters, analyzes their behaviour,
draws conclusions, formulates generalizations. What a contemporary novelist would
imply in twenty pages of description and
talk, he expresses outright in two or three
sentences that are an intellectual summing
up of all the evidence. The novelist who
employs the older method gains in definition
and clarity what he loses in realism, in life,
in expansive implication and suggestion.
There is much to be said for both methods of
presentation; most of all, perhaps, for a
Proustian combination of the two.

So much for Crébillon's method of presenting character. It is time to consider the
sort of people and the particular aspect of
their characters which he liked to present.
His heroes and heroines are the men and
women of our own favourite *dix-huitième*—
the eighteenth century whose representative
man is rather Casanova than Bach, rather the
Cardinal de Bernis than Wesley. They are
aristocrats who fill their indefinite leisure

with an amateur's interest in literature, art,
and even science (see, for the scientific interests, Cléandre's story, in *La Nuit et le Moment* of his physico-physiological argument
with Julie); with talk and social intercourse,
with gambling and country sports; and above
all, with that most perfect of time-killers,
amour. Crébillon's main, his almost exclu-
sive preoccupation is with the last of these
aristocratic amusements. And it is on his
psychology of love—of a certain kind of love
—that his claim to literary immortality must
be based.

Crébillon's special province is that obscure
borderland between soul and body, where
physiology and psychology meet and mingle
and are reciprocally complicated. It is a
province of which, during the last century
and in this country, at any rate, we have
heard but the scantiest accounts. It was
only with birth that physiology ever made
its entrance into the Victorian novel, not
with conception. In these matters, Crébillon's age was more scientific. The existence
of physiology was frankly admitted at every
stage of the reproductive process. It was
mentioned in connection with every kind of
love, from *l'amour passion* to *l'amour goût*.
It was freely discussed, and its phenomena
described, classified and explained. The re-

lations between the senses and the imagination, between love and pleasure, between desire and the affections are methodically defined in that literature of which Crébillon's stories are representative. And it is very right that they should be so defined. For no analysis of love can claim to be complete which ignores the physiological basis and accompaniment of the passion. Love, says Donne in his nearest approach to a versified epigram,

> Love's not so pure and abstract as they use
> To say, who have no mistress but their Muse.

The distinction between sacred and profane, spiritual and fleshly love is an arbitrary, gratuitous and metaphysical distinction. The most spiritual love is rooted in the flesh; the most sacred is only profane love sublimated and refined. To ignore these obvious facts is foolish and slightly dishonest. And indeed, they never have been ignored except by the psychologists of the nineteenth century. The writers of every other age have always admitted them. It was in aristocratic France, however, and during the eighteenth century, that they were most closely and accurately studied. Crébillon Fils is one of the acutest, one of the most scientific of the students.

Scientific—I apply the epithet deliberately, not vaguely and at random.   For Crébillon's attitude towards the phenomena of sex seems to me precisely that of the true scientific investigator.   It is with a mind entirely open and unbiassed that he approaches the subject.   He contrives to forget that love is a matter of the most intimate human concern, that it has been from time immemorial the subject of philosophical speculation and moral precept.   Making a clean sweep of all the prejudices, he sets to work, coolly and with detachment, as though the subject of his investigations were something as remote, as utterly divorced from good and evil as spiral nebulae, liver flukes or the aurora borealis.

Men have always tended to attribute to the objects of their intense emotions, and even to the emotions themselves, some kind of cosmical significance.   Mystics and lovers, for example, have never been content to find the justification for their feelings in the feelings themselves: they have asked us to believe that these feelings possess a universal truth value as well as, for themselves, a personal behaviour value.   And they have invented cosmogonies and metaphysical systems to justify and explain their emotional attitudes.   The fact that all these metaphysical systems are, scientifically speaking, almost certainly untrue in no way affects the value for the individual and for whole societies of the emotions and attitudes which gave them birth. Thus, mysticism will always be a beautiful and precious thing, even though it should be conclusively proved that all the philosophical systems based upon it are nonsensical. And one can be convinced of the superiority of spiritual to carnal, of "conjugial" to "scortatory" love without believing a word of Plato or Swedenborg.

In a quiet and entirely unpretentious way Crébillon was an expounder of the scientific truth about love—that its basis is physiological; that the intense and beautiful emotions which it arouses cannot be philosophically justified or explained, but should be gratefully accepted for what they are: feelings significant in themselves and of the highest practical importance for those who experience them. He is no vulgar and stupid cynic who denies the existence, because he cannot accept the current metaphysical explanation, of any feelings higher than the merely physical. "Les plaisirs gagnent toujours à être ennoblis," says Crébillon, through the mouth of the Duke in *Le Hasard au Coin du Feu*. It is the man of science who speaks, the unprejudiced observer, the accepter of facts. Pleasure is a fact; so is nobility. He admits the existence of both. Pleasure gains by being ennobled: that is the practical, experimental justification of all the high, aspiring, seemingly infinite emotions evoked by love. True, it may be objected that Crébillon gives too little space in his analysis of love to that which ennobles pleasure and too much to pleasure pure and simple. He would have been more truly scientific if he had reversed the balance; for that which ennobles is of more practical significance, both to individuals and to societies, than that which is ennobled. We may excuse him, perhaps, by supposing that, in the society in which he lived (the Pompadour was his patroness), his opportunities for observing the ennobling passions were scarce in comparison with his opportunities for observing the raw physiological material on which such passions work.

But it is foolish as well as ungrateful to criticize an author for what he has failed to achieve. The reader's business is with what the writer has done, not with what he has left undone. And Crébillon, after all, did do something which, whatever its limitations, was worth doing. What writer, for example, has spoken more acutely on the somewhat scabrous, but none the less important subject of feminine "temperament"? I cannot do better than quote a specimen of his analysis, with the generalization he draws from it. He is speaking here of a woman whose imagination is more ardent than her senses, and who, living in a society where this imagination is perpetually being fired, is for ever desperately trying to experience the pleasures of which she dreams. "Elle a l'imagination fort vive et fort déréglée, et quoique l'inutilité des épreuves qu'elle a faites en certain genre eût dû la corriger d'en faire, elle ne veut pas se persuader qu'elle soit née plus malheureuse qu'elle croit que d'autres ne le sont, et elle se flatte toujours qu'il est réservé au dernier qu'elle prend de la rendre aussi sensible qu'elle désire de l'être. Je ne doute même pas que cette idée ne soit la source de ses déréglements et de la peine qu'elle prend de jouer ce qu'elle ne sent pas. . . . Je dirai plus, c'est qu'aujourd'hui il est prouvé que ce sont les femmes à qui les plaisirs de l'amour sont les moins nécessaires qui les recherchent avec le plus de fureur, et que les trois quarts de celles qui se sont perdues avaient reçu de la nature tout ce qu'il leur fallait pour ne l'être pas." Admirable description of a type not at all uncommon in all societies where lovemaking is regarded as the proper study of womankind! The type, I repeat, is not uncommon; but Crébillon's succinct and accurate description of it is something almost unique.

Here is another passage in which he analyzes the motives of a different type of cold woman—a much more dangerous type, it may be remarked: the type to which all successful adventuresses belong. "Soit caprice, soit vanité, la chose du monde qui lui plaît le plus est d'inspirer de désirs; elle jouit du moins des transports de son amant. D'ailleurs, la froideur de ses sens n'empêche pas sa tête de s'animer, et si la nature lui a refusé ce que l'on appelle *le plaisir*, elle lui a en échange donné une sorte de volupté qui n'existe, à la vérité, que dans ses idées; mais qui lui fait peut-être éprouver quelque chose de plus délicat que ce qui ne part que des sens. Pour vous," adds Clitandre, addressing his companion, "pour vous, plus heureuse qu'elle, vous avez, si je ne me trompe, rassemblé les deux."

It would be possible to compile out of the works of Crébillon a whole collection of such character-sketches and aphorisms. "What every Young Don Juan ought to Know" might serve as title to this florilegium. It should be placed in the hands of all those, women as well as men, who propose to lead, professionally, the arduous and difficult life of leisure. Here are a few of the aphorisms which will deserve to find a place in this anthology of psychological wisdom.

"Une jolie femme dépend bien moins d'elle-même que des circonstances; et par malheur il s'en trouvé tant, de si peu prévues, de si pressantes, qu'il n'y a point à s'étonner si, après plusieurs aventures, elle n'a connu ni l'amour, ni son cœur. Il s'ensuit que ce qu'on croit la dernière fantaisie d'une femme est bien souvent sa première passion."

"Les sens ont aussi leur délicatesse; à un certain point on les émeut; qu'on le passe, on les révolte."

"L'on n'occupe pas longtemps l'imagination d'une femme sans aller jusqu'à son cœur, ou du moins sans que par les effets cela ne revienne au même."

Of Crébillon's life there is but little to say. It was quite uneventful. The record of it, singularly scanty, contains almost no unusual or surprising element. It was precisely the life which you would expect the author of *Le Sopha* to have led: a cheerful, social, literary life in the Paris of Louis XV. Crébillon was born on St. Valentine's Day, 1707, thus achieving legitimacy by fifteen days; for his parents were only married on the thirty-first of January. His father was Prosper Jolyot de Crébillon, the tragic poet

who provoked the envy and the competitive
rivalry of Voltaire. I am not ashamed to say
that I have never read a line of the elder
Crébillon's works. Life is not so long that
one can afford to spend even the briefest time
in the perusal of eighteenth-century French
tragedians. I am not even quite convinced
that it is long enough to justify one in reading those of the seventeenth century. But
let that pass. The time I have given to
Racine and Corneille has been given, in any
case, irrevocably. To Crébillon the Elder
I have so far given nothing; and I hope to
live out my days without ever allowing him
a minute, a second even, of my exiguous
treasure. So much for the genius of Crébillon père.

The literary career of the younger Crébillon began in the theatre. In association with
the actors Romagnesi, Biancolelli and Ric-
coboni he composed a number of satirical
pieces and parodies for the Italian come-
dians. It was at this period that he confided
to Sébastien Mercier, "qu'il n'avait encore
achevé la lecture des tragédies de son père,
mais que cela viendrait. Il regardait la
tragédie française comme la farce la plus
complète qu'ait pu inventer l'esprit humain."

His first successful novel, *Tanzai et Néar-
darné, Histoire Japonaise*, was published in

1734. It was so successful, indeed, and so Japanese, that Crébillon, accused of satirizing the Cardinal de Rohan and other important persons, was arrested and thrown into prison, from which, however, the good graces of a royal reader soon released him.

Tanzai was followed in 1736 by *Les Égarements du Cœur et de l'Esprit*, and in 1740 by *Le Sopha*. It was the epoch of Crébillon's social triumphs. He was for some time perpetual chairman of the famous dinners of the Caveau, and there were many other societies of which he was, officially or unofficially, the leading light.

In 1748 he married—somewhat tardily, for he had had a child by her two years before—an English wife, Lady Mary Howard. It is said that the poor lady squinted, was very ugly, awkward in society, shy and deeply religious. Crébillon seems, none the less, to have been a model husband, while the marriage lasted; which was not very long, however, for Lady Mary died about 1756. Their only child died in infancy a short time after being legitimated.

It was in 1759 that the favour of Madame de Pompadour procured for Crébillon the post of Royal Censor of Literature. He performed his duties conscientiously and to the satisfaction of all parties concerned. On the

death of his father, in 1762, he received a
pension.   In 1774 he became Police Censor
as well as Royal Censor.   In 1777 he died.
For all practical purposes, however, he had
been dead fifteen years or more.   "Il y a
longtemps," said his obituarist, "très longtemps même, qu'il avait eu le chagrin de se
voir survivre à lui-même."   Melancholy
fate!   It caused his contemporaries to do
him, towards the end, something less than
justice.   The most enthusiastic of his epi-
taphs is cool enough:

> Dans ce tombeau gît Crébillon.
> Qui? le fameux tragique?—Non!
> Celui qui le mieux peignit l'âme
> Du petit-maître et de la femme.

The praise is faint.   It is meant, perhaps, to
damn.   But it does not succeed in damning.
To have been the best painter of anybody's
soul, even the fop's, even the eighteenth-century lady's, is a fine achievement.   "Je fus
étonnée," says one of Crébillon's characters,
describing the charms of her lover's conversation, "je fus étonnée de la sorte de con-
sistance que les objets les plus frivoles sem-
blaient prendre entre ses mains."   The whole
merit of that French eighteenth century, of
which Crébillon was the representative man,
consisted precisely in giving "a sort of consistency to the most frivolous objects."   To

lead a life of leisure gracefully is an art, and though we can all do nothing, few of us contrive to do it well. It is scarcely possible to imagine a life more hopelessly futile than that which was led by the men and women of the old French aristocracy. Intrinsically, such a life seems ghastly in its emptiness and sterility. And yet, somehow, by sheer force of style, these frivolous creatures of the *dix-huitième* contrived to fill the emptiness, to coax the most charming and elegant flowers from the sterility of their existence. To the most futile of lives they gave "a sort of consistency"; they endowed nothingness with solidity and form. Crébillon shared this power with his contemporaries. The conquests of the *petit-maître*, the prompt surrenders of Célie and Cidalise and Julie— these are his theme. It seems unpromising in its smallness and its triviality. But by dint of treating it seriously—with the double seriousness of the scientific observer and the literary artist—he has made out of it something which we in our turn are compelled to take seriously. Like Célie, we are astonished.

ADVERTISEMENT

I HAVE always been interested in the subtleties of literary form. This preoccupation with the outward husk, with the letter of literature, is, I dare say, the sign of a fundamental spiritual impotence. Gigadibs, the literary man, can understand the tricks of the trade; but when it is a question, not of conjuring, but of miracles, he is no more effective than Mr. Sludge. Still, conjuring is amusing to watch and to practise; an interest in the machinery of the art requires no further justification. I have dallied with many literary forms, taking pleasure in their different intricacies, studying the means by which great authors of the past have resolved the technical problems presented by each. Sometimes I have even tried my hand at solving the problems myself—delightful and salubrious exercise for the mind. And now I have discovered the most exciting, the most arduous literary form of all, the most difficult to master, the most pregnant in curious possibilities. I mean the advertisement.

Nobody who has not tried to write an advertisement has any idea of the delights and difficulties presented by this form of literature—or shall I say of "applied literature," for the sake of those who still believe in the romantic superiority of the pure, the disinterested, over the immediately useful? The problem that confronts the writer of advertisements is an immensely complicated one, and by reason of its very arduousness immensely interesting. It is far easier to write ten passably effective Sonnets, good enough to take in the not too inquiring critic, than one effective advertisement that will take in a few thousand of the uncritical buying public. The problem presented by the Sonnet is child's play compared with the problem of the advertisement. In writing a Sonnet one need think only of oneself. If one's readers find one boring or obscure, so much the worse for them. But in writing an advertisement one must think of other people. Advertisement writers may not be lyrical, or obscure, or in any way esoteric. They must be universally intelligible. A good advertisement has this in common with drama and oratory, that it must be immediately comprehensible and directly moving. But at the same time it must possess all the succinctness of epigram.

The orator and the dramatist have "world enough and time" to produce their effects by cumulative appeals; they can turn all round their subject, they can repeat; between the heights of their eloquence they can gracefully practise the art of sinking, knowing that a period of flatness will only set off the splendour of their impassioned moments. But the advertiser has no space to spare; he pays too dearly for every inch. He must play upon the minds of his audience with a small and limited instrument. He must persuade them to part with their money in a speech that is no longer than many a lyric by Herrick. Could any problem be more fascinatingly difficult? No one should be allowed to talk about the *mot juste* or the polishing of style who has not tried his hand at writing an advertisement of something which the public does not want, but which it must be persuaded into buying. Your *boniment* must not exceed a poor hundred and fifty or two hundred words. With what care you must weigh every syllable! What infinite pains must be taken to fashion every phrase into a barbed hook that shall stick in the reader's mind and draw from its hiding-place within his pocket the reluctant coin! One's style and ideas must be lucid and simple enough to be understood by all; but, at the same time, they must not be vulgar. Elegance and an economical distinction are required; but any trace of literariness in an advertisement is fatal to its success.

I do not know whether any one has yet written a history of advertising. If the book does not already exist it will certainly have to be written. The story of the development of advertising from its infancy in the early nineteenth century to its luxuriant maturity in the twentieth is an essential chapter in the history of democracy. Advertisement begins abjectly, crawling on its belly like the serpent after the primal curse. Its abjection is the oily humbleness of the shopkeeper in an oligarchical society. Those nauseating references to the nobility and clergy, which are the very staple of early advertisements, are only possible in an age when the aristocracy and its established Church effectively ruled the land. The custom of invoking these powers lingered on long after they had ceased to hold sway. It is now, I fancy, almost wholly extinct. It may be that certain old-fashioned girls' schools still provide education for the daughters of the nobility and clergy; but I am inclined to doubt it. Advertisers still find it worth while to parade the names and escutcheons of kings. But anything less than royalty is, frankly, a "wash-out."

The crawling style of advertisement with

its mixture of humble appeals to patrons and its hyperbolical laudation of the goods advertised, was early varied by the pseudoscientific style, a simple development of the quack's patter at the fair. Balzacians will remember the advertisement composed by Finot and the Illustrious Gaudissard for César Birotteau's "Huile Céphalique." The type is not yet dead; we still see advertisements of substances "based on the principles established by the Academy of Sciences," substances known "to the ancients, the Romans, the Greeks and the nations of the North," but lost and only rediscovered by the advertiser. The style and manner of these advertisements belonging to the early and middle periods of the Age of Advertisement continue to bear the imprint of the once despicable position of commerce. They are written with the impossible and insincere unctuousness of tradesmen's letters. They are horribly uncultured; and when their writers aspire to something more ambitious than the counting-house style, they fall at once into the stilted verbiage of self-taught learning. Some of the earlier efforts to raise the tone of advertisements are very curious. One remembers those remarkable full-page advertisements of Eno's Fruit Salt, loaded with weighty apophthegms from Emerson,

Epictetus, Zeno the Eleatic, Pomponazzi, Slawkenbergius, and other founts of human wisdom. There was noble reading on these strange pages. But they shared with sermons the defect of being a little dull.

The art of advertisement writing has flowered with democracy. The lords of industry and commerce came gradually to understand that the right way to appeal to the Free Peoples of the World was familiarly, in an honest man-to-man style. They perceived that exaggeration and hyperbole do not really pay, that charlatanry must at least have an air of sincerity. They confided in the public, they appealed to its intelligence in every kind of flattering way. The technique of the art became at once immensely more difficult than it had ever been before, until now the advertisement is, as I have already hinted, one of the most interesting and difficult of modern literary forms. Its potentialities are not yet half explored. Already the most interesting and, in some cases, the only readable part of most American periodicals is the advertisement section. What does the future hold in store?

MONTESENARIO

IT was March and the snow was melting. Half wintry, half vernal, the mountain looked patchy, like a mangy dog. The southward slopes were bare; but in every hollow, on the sunless side of every tree, the snow still lay, white under the blue transparent shadows.

We walked through a little pine wood; the afternoon sunlight breaking through the dark foliage lit up here a branch, there a length of trunk, turning the ruddy bark into a kind of golden coral. Beyond the wood the hill lay bare to the summit. On the very crest a mass of buildings lifted their high sunlit walls against the pale sky, a chilly little New Jerusalem. It was the monastery of Montesenario. We climbed towards it, toilsomely; for the last stage in the pilgrim's progress from Florence to Montesenario is uncommonly steep and the motor must be left behind. And suddenly, as though to welcome us, as though to encourage our efforts, the heavenly city disgorged a troop of angels. Turning a corner of the track we saw them coming down to meet us, by two and two in a long file; angels in black cassocks with round black hats on their heads—a seminary taking its afternoon airing. They were young boys, the eldest sixteen or seventeen, the youngest not more than ten. Flapping along in their black skirts they walked with an unnatural decorum. It was difficult to believe, when one saw the little fellows at the head of the crocodile, with the tall Father in charge striding along at their side, it was difficult to believe that they were not masquerading. It seemed a piece of irreverent fun: a caricature by Goya come to life. But their faces were serious; chubby or adolescently thin, they wore already an unctuously clerical expression. It was no joke. Looking at those black-robed children, one wished that it had been.

We climbed on; the little priestlings descended out of sight. And now at last we were at the gates of the heavenly city. A little paved and parapeted platform served as landing to the flight of steps that led up into the heart of the convent. In the middle of the plaform stood a more than life-sized statue of some unheard-of saint. It was a comically admirable piece of eighteenth-century baroque. Carved with coarse brilliance, the creature gesticulated ecstatically, rolling its eyes to heaven; its garments flapped around it in broad folds. It was not, somehow, the sort of saint one expected to see standing sentinel over the bleakest hermitage in Tuscany. And the convent itself —that too seemed incongruous on the top of this icy mountain. For the heavenly city was a handsome early baroque affair with *settecento* trimmings and additions. The church was full of twiddly gilt carvings and dreadfully competent pictures; the remains of the seven pious Florentines who, in the thirteenth century, fled from the city of destruction in the plain below, and founded this hermitage on the mountain, were coffered in a large gold and crystal box, illuminated, like a show-case in the drawing-room of a collector of porcelain, by concealed electric lights. No, the buildings were ludicrous. But after all, what do buildings matter? A man can paint beautiful pictures in a slum, can write poetry in Wigan; and conversely he can live in an exquisite house, surrounded by masterpieces of ancient art, and yet (as one sees almost invariably when collectors of the antique, relying for once on their own judgment, and not on tradition, "go in for" modern art) be crassly insensitive and utterly without taste. Within certain limits, environment counts for very little. It is only when environment is extremely unfavourable that it can blast or distort the powers of the mind. And however favourable, it can do nothing to extend the limits set by nature to a man's ability. So here the architecture seemed impossibly incongruous with the bleak place, with the very notion of a hermitage; but the hermits who live in the midst of it are probably not even aware of its existence. In the shade of the absurd statue of San Filippo Benizi a Buddha would be able to think as Buddhistically as beneath the bo-tree.

In the grounds of the monastery we saw half a dozen black-frocked Servites sawing wood—sawing with vigour and humility, in spite of the twiddly gilding in the church and the *settecento* bell tower. They looked the genuine article. And the view from the mountain's second peak was in the grandest eremitic tradition. The hills stretched away as far as the eye could reach into the wintry haze, like a vast heaving sea frozen to stillness. The valleys were filled with blue shadow, and all the sunward slopes were the colour of rusty gold. At our feet the ground fell away into an immense blue gulf. The gauzy air softened every outline, smoothed away every detail, leaving only golden lights and violet shadows floating like the disembodied essence of a landscape, under the pale sky.

We stood for a long time looking out over that kingdom of silence and solemn beauty. The solitude was as profound as the shadowy gulf beneath us; it stretched to the misty horizons and up into the topless sky. Here at the heart of it, I thought, a man might begin to understand something about that part of his being which does not reveal itself in the quotidian commerce of life; which the social contacts do not draw forth, spark-like, from the sleeping flint that is an untried spirit; that part of him, of whose very existence he is only made aware in solitude and silence. And if there happens to be no silence in his life, if he is never solitary, then he may go down to his grave without a knowledge of its existence, much less an understanding of its nature or realization of its potentialities.

We retraced our steps to the monastery and thence walked down the steep path to the motor. A mile farther down the road towards Pratolino, we met the priestlings returning from their walk. Poor children! But was their lot worse, I wondered, than that of the inhabitants of the city in the valley? On their mountain top they lived under a tyrannous rule, they were taught to believe in a number of things manifestly silly. But was the rule any more tyrannous than that of the imbecile conventions which control the lives of social beings in the plain? Was snobbery about duchesses and distinquished novelists more reasonable than snobbery about Jesus Christ and the Saints? Was hard work to the greater glory of God more detestable than eight hours a day in an office for the greater enrichment of the Jews? Temperance was a bore, no doubt; but was it so nauseatingly wearisome as excess? And the expense of spirit in prayer and meditation—was that so much less amusing than the expense of spirit in a waste of shame? Driving down towards the city in the plain, I wondered. And when, in the Via Tornabuoni, we passed Mrs. Thingummy, in the act of laboriously squeezing herself out on to the pavement through the door of her gigantic limousine, I suddenly and perfectly understood what it was that had made those seven rich Florentine merchants, seven hundred years ago, abandon their position in the world, and had sent them up into the high wilderness, to live in holes at the top of Montesenario. I looked back; Mrs. Thingummy was waddling across the pavement into the jeweller's shop. Yes, I perfectly understood.

EUPHUES REDIVIVUS

I HAVE recently been fortunate in securing a copy of that very rare and precious novel *Delina Delaney*, by Amanda M. Ros, authoress of *Irene Iddesleigh* and *Poems of Puncture*. Mrs. Ros's name is only known to a small and select band of readers. But by these few she is highly prized; one of her readers, it is said, actually was at the pains to make a complete manuscript copy of *Delina Delaney*, so great was his admiration and so hopelessly out of print the book. Let me recommend the volume, Mrs. Ros's masterpiece, to the attention of enterprising publishers.

Delina Delaney opens with a tremendous, an almost, in its richness of vituperative eloquence, Rabelaisian denunciation of Mr. Barry Pain, who had, it seems, treated *Irene Iddesleigh* with scant respect in his review of the novel in *Black and White*. "This so-called Barry Pain, by name, has taken upon himself to criticize a work, the depth of which fails to reach the solving power of his borrowed, and, he'd have you believe, varied talent." But "I care not for the opinion of half-starved upstarts, who don the garb of a shabby-genteel, and fain would feed the mind of the people with the worthless scraps of stolen fancies." So perish all reviewers! And now for Delina herself.

The story is a simple one. Delina Delaney, daughter of a fisherman, loves and is loved by Lord Gifford. The baleful influence of a dark-haired Frenchwoman, Madame de Maine, daughter of the Count-av-Nevo, comes between the lovers and their happiness, and Delina undergoes fearful torments, including three years' penal servitude, before their union can take place. It is the manner, rather than the matter, of the book which is remarkable. Here, for instance, is a fine conversation between Lord Gifford and his mother, an aristocratic dame who strenuously objects to his connection with Delina. Returning one day to Columba Castle she hears an unpleasant piece of news: her son has been seen kissing Delina in the conservatory.

" 'Home again, mother?' he boldly uttered, as he gazed reverently in her face.

" 'Home to Hades!' returned the raging high-bred daughter of distinguished effeminacy.

" 'Ah me! what is the matter?' meekly inquired his lordship.

" 'Everything is the matter with a broken-hearted mother of low-minded offspring,' she answered hotly. . . . 'Henry Edward Ludlow Gifford, son of my strength, idolized remnant of my inert husband, who at this moment invisibly offers the scourging whip of fatherly authority to your backbone of resentment (though for years you think him dead to your movements) and pillar of maternal trust.' "

Poor Lady Gifford! her son's behaviour was her undoing. The shock caused her to lose first her reason and then her life. Her son was heart-broken at the thought that he was responsible for her downfall:

" 'Is it true, O Death,' I cried in my agony, 'that you have wrested from me my mother, Lady Gifford of Columba Castle, and left me here, a unit figuring on the great blackboard of the past, the shaky surface of the present and fickle field of the future to track my life-steps, with gross indifference to her wished-for wish?' . . . Blind she lay to the presence of her son, who charged her death-gun with the powder of accelerated wrath.' "

It is impossible to suppose that Mrs. Ros can ever have read *Euphues* or the earlier romances of Robert Greene. How then shall we account for the extraordinary resemblance to Euphuism of her style? how explain those rich alliterations, those elaborate "kennings" and circumlocutions of which the fabric of her book is woven? Take away from Lyly his erudition and his passion for antithesis, and you have Mrs. Ros. Delina is own sister to Euphues and Pandosta. The fact is that Mrs. Ros happens, though separated from Euphuism by three hundred years and more, to have arrived independently at precisely the same stage of development as Lyly and his disciples. It is possible to see in a growing child a picture in miniature of all the phases through which humanity has passed in its development. And, in the same way, the mind of an individual (especially when that individual has been isolated from the main current of contemporary thought) may climb, alone, to a point at which, in the past, a whole generation has rested. In Mrs. Ros we see, as we see in the Elizabethan novelists, the result of the discovery of art by an unsophisticated mind and of its first conscious attempt to produce the artistic. It is remarkable how late in the history of every literature simplicity is invented. The first attempts of any people to be consciously literary are always productive of the most elaborate artificiality. Poetry is always written before prose and always in a language as remote as possible from the language of ordinary life. The language and versification of *Beowulf* are far more artificial and remote from life than those of, say, *The Rape of the Lock*. The Euphuists were not barbarians making their first discovery of literature; they were, on the contrary, highly educated. But in one thing they were unsophisticated: they were discovering prose. They were realizing that prose could be written with art, and they wrote it as artificially as they possibly could, just as their Saxon ancestors wrote poetry. They became intoxicated with their discovery of artifice. It was some time before the intoxication wore off and men saw that art was possible without artifice. Mrs. Ros, an Elizabethan born out of her time, is still under the spell of that magical and delicious intoxication.

Mrs. Ros's artifices are often more remarkable and elaborate even than Lyly's. This is how she tells us that Delina earned money by doing needlework:

"She tried hard to keep herself a stranger to her poor old father's slight income by the use of the finest production of steel, whose blunt edge eyed the reely covering with marked greed, and offered its sharp dart to faultless fabrics of flaxen fineness."

And Lord Gifford parts from Delina in these words:

"I am just in time to hear the toll of a parting bell strike its heavy weight of appalling softness against the weakest fibres of a heart of love, arousing and tickling its dormant action, thrusting the dart of evident separation deeper into its tubes of tenderness, and fanning the flame, already unextinguishable, into volumes of burning blaze."

But more often Mrs. Ros does not exceed the bounds which Lyly set for himself. Here, for instance, is a sentence that might have come direct out of *Euphues:*

"Two days after, she quit Columba Castle and resolved to enter the holy cloisters of a convent, where, she believed she'd be dead to the built hopes of wealthy worth, the crooked steps to worldly distinction, and the designing creaks [*sic*] in the muddy stream of love."

Or again, this description of the artful charmers who flaunt along the streets of London is written in the very spirit and language of *Euphues:*

"Their hair was a light-golden colour, thickly fringed in front, hiding in many cases the furrows of a life of vice; behind, reared coils, some of which differed in hue, exhibiting the fact that they were on patrol for the price of another supply of dye. . . . The elegance of their attire had the glow of robbery—the rustle of many a lady's silent curse. These tools of brazen effrontery were strangers to the blush of innocence that tinged many a cheek, as they would gather round some of God's ordained, praying in flowery words of decoying Cockney, that they should break their holy vows by accompanying them to the halls of adultery. Nothing daunted at the staunch refusal of different divines, whose modest walk was interrupted by their bold assertion of loathsome rights, they moved on, while laughs of hidden rage and defeat flitted across their doll-decked faces, to die as they next accosted some rustic-looking critics, who, tempted with their polished twang, their earnest advances, their pitiful entreaties, yielded, in their ignorance of the ways of a large city, to their glossy offers, and accompanied, with slight hesitation, these artificial shells of immorality to their homes of ruin, degradation and shame."

BELLO BELLO

THE word "beautiful" comes rarely to English lips. It is too long, too serious, a little foreign-sounding for our native taste. Uttering those three syllables we seem to be committing ourselves too irrevocably to a serious opinion; and we are chary of that, much too chary. Beautiful—it sounds high-brow, it suggests long hair; we are almost ashamed of saying it. It is only on solemn and rather tremendous occasions—on Sundays, so to speak, and not on common days—that an Englishman permits himself to pronounce so dangerous a word. Our ancestors' safer and more English monosyllable, "fair," has sadly come down in the world. The only beautiful thing that we still call fair is the weather. For the rest, it is now all but a term of denigration; it damns with faint praise. Restore to "fair" its original meaning, and Englishmen would no longer be chary of calling beauty by its name. It is only the formidable high-brow word, with its philosophical associations, that we are afraid of. To-day the national epithet of approbation is "nice"—shrilling up in more emotional moments to "lovely." The fair maid of Perth is now a lovely Scotch girl, and many men so beautiful, a nice-looking lot.

More fortunate in this respect than we are, the Italians, when they talk of beauty, suffer from no inhibitions. Their word for "beautiful" is ancient and thoroughly native. *Bello* is as little highbrow as was our "fair." It suggests nothing philosophical or religious. The ghosts of Good and True march dimly behind our Beautiful. But *bello* is a peasant's word of which nobody need be ashamed, even if it does also happen to be Dante's word. *Bello*—it is the favourite national adjective; no word is oftener uttered. *Bello bello*—they love to double it, to put both barrels, bang! bang! left and right, into the same bird. *Bello bello* and then *bellissimo*, the *coup de grâce* with the butt-end while the bird is still struggling on the ground.

Bello, *bellissimo*, *bellezza:* the words beset Italian conversation. From a cornice by Michelangelo to a *bel paese* cheese or the most horrible dribbling baby, everything is beautiful. Is it in England that a political party would select as its battle-cry, "Youth, youth, spring-time of beauty"? But the Fascisti marched on Rome—or mostly, rather, went by train—to the tune of *"Giovinezza, giovinezza, primavera di belle-e-e-ez-za!"* And it would certainly have been

difficult to find a set of young men less high-
brow than the Fascists, less long-haired—
spiritually long-haired, I mean; for physi-
cally long-haired the Black Shirts mostly were
at that time, though the fashion has changed
since then, with frizzy locks rising, perpendicular and stiff, six or seven inches into the
air, for the sake, it was said, of looking *più
terribili*. Not since Trafalgar has beauty
figured in an English patriotic song, and even
here the third person in the trinity, "England, Home and Beauty," seems to have got
there more by accident, and because England
expected every man to do his duty, than by
deliberate design. The exigencies of rhyme
are for ever incongruously coupling the Lady
Beauty with the stern Daughter of the Voice
of God. But in Italian, where every word
rhymes with almost every other, the poet's
hand is rarely forced, and if the Fascists sing
of beauty when they march, it is because they
like to, not because there are no other rhymes
to youth.

Since *bello*, then, is the favourite Italian
adjective, it would be natural to suppose that
beauty was a quality in their surroundings to
which the Italians attached great value.
That they did so is sufficiently obvious; but
that they do not is not, alas! quite so clear.
Signor Ugo Ojetti, indeed, has roundly de-

clared that the Italians to-day have, as a people, the worst taste of any in Europe. And certainly, when one looks at the modern *villini* on the outskirts of Italian towns, when one sees the furniture, the fabrics, the pictures and statuary they contain, one can believe that Signor Ojetti may perhaps be right.

For if *bello* is the Italian's favourite adjective, there is another that runs it very close in popularity: *moderno*. The Italians only ecstatically say *bello;* but *moderno* they really mean. And it appears to be impossible for a thing to possess both these qualities, in Italy at any rate, at the same time. Italy, the brand-new country that has only existed since 1870, is still too busy developing her material resources to be practically concerned with the reconciliation of *bello* (as the old Italians understood *bello*) with *moderno*. There are still too many waterfalls to be harnessed, too many power-stations and factories to be built, for the Italians to do much but talk about the *bello*. The people with the oldest and most splendid civilization in Europe are now in some ways younger than the Americans of a generation ago. They have grown into a kind of second boyhood when nothing matters but engines and motor-cars. The vitality, intelligence and energy of which in the past so much went into the creation of those works of art which, with the hotels, now constitute the necessary plant of the tourist industry, are still there; but they seem to have been deflected into other channels. But perhaps when the country has been made sufficiently *moderno*, its people will find the leisure to think of a new *bellezza*.

It is interesting, meanwhile, to see what does pass for artistically beautiful among the modernities. Signor Ojetti has complained that Italian bad taste is worse than the bad taste of other countries because it is less consistent and systematic. It is a bad taste of shreds and patches. But it seems to me that all contemporary manifestations of the *bello* in Italy, however different the conventions in terms of which they are executed, have always one thing in common: they are all fundamentally baroque. The model may be Bernini or Mestrovic, the convention may be one of extreme realism or geometrical simplification; it does not matter. In every work one sees that same baroque violence which defeats its own object, the emotionalism which does not move, the straining after effect which achieves nothing, the gesticulating sublime which is ridiculous. *Bello* in the twentieth century is a throaty music, is pages of d'Annunzio's clotted and feverish verbiage. *Bello-cum-moderno* manifests itself in the Victor Emanuel monument in Rome (not half bad, after all, if you leave the statues out, in the theatrical seventeenth-century manner); in the Centro della Città in Florence; in projects for war memorials conceived in the most powerful Munich style. By some strange and malignant fate the Italians, whose *bello* was once so sober and intellectual in its moving passion, seem to have got permanently bogged among the facile emotionalisms and violences of the seventeenth century. Palestrina was once a representative Italian artist; to-day it is Puccini.

There is no reason to suppose that the Italian character has fundamentally changed in recent centuries. The qualities which, in baroque art, reveal themselves as violence and emotionalism were always there, but kept down, but tempered and severely moulded by the intellect. The most moving works of art are always those in which passion is confined within a severe formal scheme. The artists of the seventeenth century hoped, by throwing off formal restraint, by exploiting technical resources to their utmost limit, to make their works more moving and passionate. They

achieved the exact opposite; and, compared
with the works of the fifteenth and sixteenth
centuries, theirs are uninteresting and even,
positively, unexciting. The *bello* of to-day,
being still further from the great tradition,
is still less interesting.

Why the great tradition, the remains of
which persisted, after all, till the end of the
eighteenth century, should so miserably have
perished in Italy, even as it did in our comparatively benighted England, is a great
mystery. Mysterious, too, is the modern
Italian tendency to prefer the worst foreign
conventions to their own best. The Italian
craftsman has all the skill he ever possessed;
but if you ask a house-painter to decorate
your house for you, his first instinct will be to
cover your walls with all the horrible decorative shapes invented in Munich or Vienna
during the last five-and-twenty years. But
in this the Italian is not unique. The Chinese, it is said, are now ashamed of their
ancient art, and prefer a coloured supple-
ment by Mr. Barribal to the finest work of
painters ignorant of chiaroscuro and the laws
of perspective. That we needs must love
the highest when we see it is not, alas! invariably true. When a great tradition fails
and grows tired through lack of great men
to continue and develop it, when there are

only second-rate artists repeating competently what has been done before, then a new and strikingly bad style—the important thing is that it should be striking—will come as a revelation, and we rush, in a delirious Gadarene descent, headlong towards the lowest. It is unlikely that Art Nouveau would have had much success in Rome during the lifetimes of Raphael and Michelangelo. And, conversely, *bello-moderno* will begin to mean something different from baroque emotionalism as soon as a few more artists of genius make their appearance upon the Italian scene.

VIEWS OF HOLLAND

I HAVE always been rather partial to
plane geometry; probably because it was
the only branch of mathematics that was
ever taught me in such a way that I could
understand it. For though I have no belief
in the power of education to turn public
school boys into Newtons (it being quite
obvious that, whatever opportunity may be
offered, it is only those rare beings desirous
of learning and possessing a certain amount
of native ability who ever do learn anything), yet I must insist, in my own defence,
that the system of mathematical instruction
of which, at Eton, I was the unfortunate
victim, was calculated not merely to turn my
desire to learn into stubborn passive resistance, but also to stifle whatever rudimentary
aptitude in this direction I might have possessed. But let that pass. Suffice to say
that, in spite of my education and my con-
genital ineptitude, plane geometry has always charmed me by its simplicity and ele-
grance, its elimination of detail and the
individual case, its insistence on generalities.

My love for plane geometry prepared me
to feel a special affection for Holland. For

the Dutch landscape has all the qualities that make geometry so delightful. A tour in Holland is a tour through the first books of Euclid. Over a country that is the ideal plane surface of the geometry books, the roads and the canals trace out the shortest distances between point and point. In the interminable polders, the road-topped dykes and gleaming ditches intersect one another at right angles, a criss-cross of perfect parallels. Each rectangle of juicy meadowland contained between the intersecting dykes has identically the same area. Five kilometres long, three deep—the figures record themselves on the clock face of the cyclometer. Five by three by—how many? The demon of calculation possesses the mind. Rolling along those smooth brick roads between the canals, one strains one's eyes to count the dykes at right angles and parallel to one's own. One calculates the area of the polders they enclose. So many square kilometres. But the square kilometres have to be turned into acres. It is a fearful sum to do in one's head; the more so as one has forgotten how many square yards there are in an acre.

And all the time, as one advances the huge geometrical landscape spreads out on either side of the car like an opening fan. Along the level sky-line a score of windmills wave

their arms like dancers in a geometrical ballet.   Ineluctably, the laws of perspective
lead away the long roads and shining waters
to a misty vanishing point.   Here and there
—mere real irrelevancies in the midst of this
ideal plain—a few black and white cows out
of a picture by Cuyp browse indefatigably in
the lush green grass or, remembering Paul
Potter, mirror themselves like so many
ruminating Narcissi, in the waters of a canal.
Sometimes one passes a few human beings,
deplorably out of place, but doing their best,
generally, to make up for their ungeometrical
appearance by mounting bicycles.   The cir-
cular wheels suggest a variety of new
theorems and a new task for the demon of
calculation.   Suppose the radius of the
wheels to be fifteen inches; then fifteen times
fifteen times *pi* will be the area.   The only
trouble is that one has forgotten the value
of *pi*.

Hastily I exorcise the demon of calculation that I may be free to admire the farmhouse on the opposite bank of the canal on
our right.   How perfectly it fits into the
geometrical scheme!   On a cube, cut down
to about a third of its height, is placed a tall
pyramid.   That is the house.   A plantation
of trees, set in quincunx formation, surrounds it; the limits of its rectangular garden

are drawn in water on the green plain, and beyond these neat ditches extend the interminable flat fields.   There are no outhouses, no barns, no farm-yard with untidy stacks. The hay is stored under the huge pyramidal roof, and in the truncated cube below live, on one side the farmer and his family, on the other side (during winter only; for during the rest of the year they sleep in the fields) his black and white Cuyp cows.   Every farmhouse in North Holland conforms to this type, which is traditional, and so perfectly fitted to the landscape that it would have been impossible to devise anything more suitable.   An English farm with its ranges of straggling buildings, its untidy yard, full of animals, its haystacks and pigeon-cotes, would be horribly out of place here.   In the English landscape, which is all accidents, variety, detail and particular cases, it is perfect.   But here, in this generalized and Euclidean North Holland, it would be a blot and a discord.   Geometry calls for geometry; with a sense of the aesthetic proprieties which one cannot too highly admire, the Dutch have responded to the appeal of the landscape and have dotted the plane surface of their country with cubes and pyramids.

Delightful landscape!   I know of no

country that it is more mentally exhilarating to travel in. No wonder Descartes preferred the Dutch to any other scene. It is the rationalist's paradise. One feels as one flies along in the teeth of one's own forty-mile-an-hour wind like a Cartesian Encyclopaedist—flushed with mental intoxication, convinced that Euclid is absolute reality, that God is a mathematician, that the universe is a simple affair that can be explained in terms of physics and mechanics, that all men are equally endowed with reason and that it is only a question of putting the right arguments before them to make them see the error of their ways and to inaugurate the reign of justice and common sense. Those were noble and touching dreams, commendable inebriations! We are soberer now. We have learnt that nothing is simple and rational except what we ourselves have invented; that God thinks in terms neither of Euclid nor of Riemann; that science has "explained" nothing; that the more we know the more fantastic the world becomes and the profounder the surrounding darkness; that reason is unequally distributed; that instinct is the sole source of action; that prejudice is incomparably stronger than argument, and that even in the twentieth century men behave as they did in the caves of

Altamira and in the lake dwellings of Glastonbury. And symbolically one makes the same discoveries in Holland. For the polders are not unending, nor all the canals straight, nor every house a wedded cube and pyramid, nor even the fundamental plane surface invariably plane. That delightful "Last Ride Together" feeling that fills one as one rolls along the brick-topped dykes between the canals is deceptive. The present is not eternal; the "Last Ride" through plane geometry comes to a sudden end—in a town, in forests, in the sea coast, in a winding river or great estuary. It matters little which; all are fundamentally ungeometrical; each has power to dissipate in an instant all those "paralogisms of rationalism" (as Professor Rougier calls them) which we have so fondly cherished among the polders. The towns have crooked streets thronged with people; the houses are of all shapes and sizes. The coast-line is not straight nor regularly curved, and its dunes or its dykes (for it must be defended against the besieging waves by art if not by nature) rear themselves inexcusably out of the plane surface. The woods are unscientific in their shady mysteriousness and one cannot see them for all their individual trees. The rivers are tortuous and alive with boats and barges. The inlets of the sea

are entirely shapeless. It is the real world
again after the ideal—hopelessly diversified,
complex and obscure; but, when the first re-
grets are over, equally charming with the
geometrical landscape we have left behind.
We shall find it more charming, indeed, if
our minds are practical and extroverted.
Personally, I balance my affections. For I
love the inner world as much as the outer.
When the outer vexes me, I retire to the
rational simplicities of the inner—to the
polders of the spirit. And when, in their
turn, the polders seem unduly flat, the roads
too straight and the laws of perspective too
tyrannous, I emerge again into the pleasing
confusion of untempered reality.

And how beautiful, how curious in Holland that confusion is! I think of Rotterdam
with its enormous river and its great bridges,
so crowded with the traffic of a metropolis
that one has to wait in files, half a mile long,
for one's turn to cross. I think of The Hague
and how it tries to be elegant and only succeeds in being respectable and upper middle
class; of Delft, the commercial city of three
hundred years ago; of Haarlem where, in
autumn, you see them carting bulbs as in
other countries they cart potatoes; of Hoorn
on the Zuyder Zee, with its little harbour
and seaward-looking castle, its absurd mu-

seum filled with rich mixed rubbish, its huge
storehouse of cheeses, like an old-fashioned
arsenal, where the workmen are busy all day
long polishing the yellow cannon balls on a
kind of lathe and painting them bright pink
with an aniline stain. I think of Volendam
—one line of wooden houses perched on the
sea-wall, and another line crouching in the
low green fields behind the dyke. The people at Volendam are dressed as for a musical
comedy—*Miss Hook of Holland*—the men
in baggy trousers and short jackets, the women in winged white caps, tight bodices, and
fifteen superimposed petticoats. Five thousand tourists come daily to look at them; but
they still, by some miracle, retain their inde-
pendence and self-respect. I think of Amsterdam; the old town, like a livelier Bruges,
mirrors its high brick houses in the canals.
In one quarter an enormous courtesan sits
smiling at every window, the meatiest specimens of humanity I ever saw. At nine in the
morning, at lunch-time, at six in the afternoon, the streets are suddenly filled with
three hundred thousand bicycles; every one,
in Amsterdam, goes to and from his business
on a pair of wheels. For the pedestrian as
well as for the motorist it is a nightmare.
And they are all trick cyclists. Children of
four carry children of three on their handle-

bars.   Mothers pedal gaily along with
month-old infants sleeping in cradles fastened to the back carrier.   Messenger boys
think nothing of taking two cubic metres of
parcels.   Dairymen do their rounds on bicycles specially constructed to accommodate
two hundred quart bottles of milk in a tray
between the two wheels.   I have seen nursery
gardeners carrying four palms and a dozen of
potted chrysanthemums on their handle-bars.
I have seen five people riding through the
traffic on one machine.   The most daring
feats of the circus and the music hall are part
of the quotidian routine in Amsterdam.

I think of the dunes near Schoorl.   Seen
from a little distance across the plain they
look like a range of enormous mountains
against the sky.   Following with the eye
that jagged silhouette one can feel all the
emotions aroused, shall we say, by the spectacle of the Alps seen from Turin.   The
dunes are grand; one could write a canto
from *Childe Harold* about them.   And then,
unfortunately, one realizes what for a moment one had forgotten, that this line of
formidable peaks is not looking down at one
from fifty miles away, over the curving flank
of the planet: it is just a furlong distant, and
the chimneys of the houses at its base reach
nearly two-thirds of the way to the top.   But

what does that matter? With a little good will, I insist, one can feel in Holland all the emotions appropriate to Switzerland.

Yes, they are grand, the dunes of Schoorl and Groet. But I think the grandest sight I saw in non-geometrical Holland was Zaandam—Zaandam from a distance, across the plain.

We had been driving through the polders and the open country of North Holland. Zaandam was the first piece of ungeometrical reality since Alkmaer. Technically, Zaandam is not picturesque; the guide-book has little to say about it. It is a port and manufacturing town on the Zaan, a few miles north of Amsterdam; that is all. They make cocoa there and soap. The air at Zaandam is charged in alternative strata with delicious vapours of molten chocolate and the stench of boiling fat. In wharves by the shores of the river they store American grain and timber from the Baltic. It was the granaries that first announced, from a distance, the presence of Zaandam. Like the cathedrals of a new religion, yet unpreached, they towered up into the hazy autumn air—huge oblongs of concrete set on end, almost windowless, smooth and blankly grey. It was as though their whole force were directed vertically upwards; to look from windows horizontally across the world would have been a distraction; eyes were sacrificed to this upward purpose. And the direction of that purpose was emphasized by the lines of the alternately raised and lowered panels into which the wall spaces of the great buildings were divided—long fine lines of shadow running up unbrokenly through a hundred feet from base to summit. The builders of the papal palace at Avignon used a very similar device to give their castle its appearance of enormous height and formidable impendence. The raised panel and the shallow blind arches, impossibly long in the leg, with which they variegated the surface of the wall, impart to the whole building an impetuous upward tendency. It is the same with the grain elevators at Zaandam. In the haze of autumnal Holland I remembered Provence. And I remembered, as I watched those towering shapes growing larger and larger as we approached, Chartres and Bourges and Reims: gigantic silhouettes seen at the end of a day's driving, towards evening, against a pale sky, with the little lights of a city about their base.

But if at a distance Zaandam, by its commercial monuments, reminds one of Provençal castles and the Gothic cathedrals of France, a nearer view proclaims it to be unequivocally Dutch. At the foot of the elevators and the only less enormous factories, in the atmosphere of chocolate and soap, lies the straggling town. The suburbs are long, but narrow; for they cling precariously to a knife-edge of land between two waters. The houses are small, made of wood and gaudily painted; with gardens as large as table-cloths, beautifully kept and filled—at any rate at the season when I saw them— with plushy begonias. In one, as large, in this case, as two table-cloths, were no less than fourteen large groups of statuary. In the streets are men in wooden shoes, smoking. Dogs drawing carts with brass pots in them. Innumerable bicycles. It is the real and not the ideal geometrical Holland, crowded, confusing, various, odd, charming. . . . But I sighed as we entered the town. The "Last Ride Together" was over; the dear paralogisms of rationalism were left behind. It was now necessary to face the actual world of men—and to face it, in my case, with precisely five words of Dutch (and patois at that) learned years before for the benefit of a Flemish servant: "Have you fed the cat?" No wonder I regretted the polders.

EDWARD LEAR

THERE are few writers whose works I care to read more than once, and one of them is certainly Edward Lear. Nonsense, like poetry, to which it is closely allied, like philosophic speculation, like every product of the imagination, is an assertion of man's spiritual freedom in spite of all the oppression of circumstance. As long as it remains possible for the human mind to invent the Quangle Wangle and the Fimble Fowl, to wander at will over the Great Gromboolian Plain and the hills of the Chankly Bore, the victory is ours. The existence of nonsense is the nearest approach to a proof of that unprovable article of faith, whose truth we must all assume or perish miserably: that life is worth living. It is when circumstances combine to prove, with syllogistic cogency, that life is not worth living that I turn to Lear and find comfort and refreshment. I read him and I perceive that it is a good thing to be alive; for I am free, with Lear, to be as inconsequent as I like.

Lear is a genuine poet. For what is his nonsense except the poetical imagination a little twisted out of its course? Lear had the true poet's feeling for words—words in themselves, precious and melodious, like phrases of music; personal as human beings. Marlowe talks of entertaining divine Zenocrate; Milton of the leaves that fall in Vallombrosa; Lear of the Fimble Fowl with a corkscrew leg, of runcible spoons, of things meloobious and genteel. Lewis Carroll wrote nonsense by exaggerating sense—a too logical logic. His coinages of words are intellectual. Lear, more characteristically a poet, wrote nonsense that is an excess of imagination, coined words for the sake of their colour and sound alone. His is the purer nonsense, because more poetical. Change the key ever so little and the "Dong with a Luminous Nose" would be one of the most memorable romantic poems of the nineteenth century. Think, too, of that exquisite "Yonghy Bonghy Bo"! In one of Tennyson's later volumes there is a charming little lyric about Catullus, which begins:

> Row us out from Desenzano,
>   To your Sirmione row!
> So they row'd, and there we landed—
>   *O venusta Sirmio!*

Can one doubt for a moment that he was thinking, when he wrote these words, of that superb stanza with which the "Yonghy Bonghy" opens:

> On the coast of Coromandel,
> Where the early pumpkins blow,
> In the middle of the woods,
> Dwelt the Yonghy Bonghy Bo.

Personally, I prefer Lear's poem; it is the richer and the fuller of the two.

Lear's genius is at its best in the Nonsense Rhymes, or Limericks, as a later generation has learned to call them. In these I like to think of him not merely as a poet and a draughtsman—and how unique an artist the recent efforts of Mr. Nash to rival him have only affirmed—but also as a profound social philosopher. No study of Lear would be complete without at least a few remarks on "They" of the Nonsense Rhymes. "They" are the world, the man in the street; "They" are what the leader-writers in the twopenny press would call all Right-Thinking Men and Women; "They" are Public Opinion. The Nonsense Rhymes are, for the most part, nothing more nor less than episodes selected from the history of that eternal struggle between the genius or the eccentric and his fellow-beings. Public Opinion universally abhors eccentricity. There was, for example, that charming Old Man of Melrose who walked on the tips of his toes. But "They" said (with their usual inability to appreciate the artist), "It ain't pleasant to see you at present, you stupid old man of Melrose. Occasionally, when the eccentric happens to be a criminal genius, "They" are doubtless right. The Old Man with a Gong who bumped on it all the day long deserves to be smashed. (But "They" also smashed a quite innocuous Old Man of Whitehaven merely for dancing a quadrille with a raven.) And there was that Old Person of Buda, whose conduct grew ruder and ruder; "They" were justified, I dare say, in using a hammer to silence his clamour. But it raises the whole question of punishment and of the relation between society and the individual.

When "They" are not offensive, they content themselves with being foolishly inquisitive. Thus, "They" ask the Old Man of the Wrekin whether his boats are made of leather. "They" pester the Old Man in a Tree with imbecile questions about the Bee which so horribly bored him. In these encounters the geniuses and the eccentrics often get the better of the gross and heavy-witted public. The Old Person of Ware who rode on the back of a bear certainly scored off "Them." For when "They" asked, "Does it trot?" he replied, "It does not."

(The picture shows it galloping *ventre à terre*.) "It's a Moppsikon Floppsikon bear." Sometimes, too, the eccentric actually leads "Them" on to their discomfiture. One thinks of that Old Man in a Garden, who always begged every one's pardon. When "They" asked him, What for? he replied, "You're a bore, and I trust you'll go out of my garden." But they probably ended up by smashing him.

Occasionally the men of genius adopt a Mallarméen policy. They flee from the gross besetting crowd.

> La chair est triste, hélas, et j'ai lu tous les livres.
> Fuir, là-bas, fuir. . . .

It was surely with these words on his lips that the Old Person of Bazing (whose presence of mind, for all that he was a Symbolist, was amazing) went out to purchase the steed which he rode at full speed and escaped from the people of Bazing. He chose the better part; for it is almost impossible to please the mob. The Old Person of Ealing was thought by his suburban neighbours to be almost devoid of good feeling, because, if you please, he drove a small gig with three owls and a pig. And there was that pathetic Old Man of Thermopylae (for whom I have a peculiar sympathy, since he reminds me so poignantly of myself) who never did anything properly. "They" said, "If you choose to boil eggs in your shoes, you shall never remain in Thermopylae." The sort of people "They" like do the stupidest things, have the vulgarest accomplishments. Of the Old Person of Filey his acquaintance was wont to speak highly because he danced perfectly well to the sound of a bell. And the people of Shoreham adored that fellow-citizen of theirs whose habits were marked by decorum and who bought an umbrella and sate in the cellar. Naturally; it was only to be expected.

BALLET IN CRITICISM:

SCRIABINE, OR THE VOLUPTUOUS DENTIST BALLET TO THE MUSIC OF SCRIABINE'S "PROMETHEUS"

A DENTIST'S operating chamber. The chair is placed in the centre of the stage, on a high dais approached by steps from all four sides. A carpet of rich magenta plush covers the dais, and the black chair is upholstered in the same material. The backcloth is of watered orange silk. A row of nautch girls forms a dado to this sumptuous wall. They remain at their post throughout the whole scene, swaying a little from side to side and making with their arms the movement of seaweed stirring languidly in a subaqueous wind. Their torsos, meanwhile, are in a state of unremitting tremolo: it is the well-known Dance of the Seven Stomachs. They wear bejewelled *reggipetti* of pure gold, and over their bent knees their skirts are Javanese in contour.

From the ceiling a thick black cable hangs in a graceful and sinister catenary, like a rope in one of Piranesi's prisons; it has, one clearly sees, something to do with the dentist's drill.

The music strikes up—"Prometheus," the Poem of Fire—and from either side of the stage three female acrobats, carrying enormously magnified versions of those bright steel prods and probes of the dentist's armoury, rush in. From the waist downwards they wear pink fleshings; from the waist upwards they are trained nurses, collared, cuffed and capped. It is they who record the Dentist's appointments, bring restoratives to fainting patients and cut the little gags of lint against the moment of stopping. With the first bars, then, in they rush. Against the slowly swaying, the tremulously palpitating background of the nautch girls, agile and acrobatic, they dance. The dance works up to a culmination, when the leader of the troop skips up on the dais, drives the end of her probe into an eyelet hole in front of the chair, throws up her legs and remains balanced, head downwards, her hands resting on a cross-piece at the top of the probe, her back—the fleshings above, the nurse's collar below—presented to the audience; while her five companions, with an ever-increasing velocity, with vaster and ever vaster bounds, go pole-jumping on their shining prods round and round the dais, like a troop of lady bullfighters, tight-waisted and with long, pink, tapering legs, vaulting from between the horns of the charging beast in the royal bull-ring of Cnossos.

The dance disintegrates, the balancer on the dais comes tumbling with a studied grace to earth, and the troop manœuvres into open formation on one side of the stage.

Shot from a spring-board in the opposite wings, the *premier danseur* enters like a flying saint in a picture by Tintoretto. It is the Dentist. He wears a black alpaca jacket and tight check trousers. Above the collar a great false head of wax. Across the cranial hemisphere, seventeen long black hairs are drawn, arachnean bridges between the curly tufts above the ears. The mask is quite featureless, a pink blank with belly high lights; there is only a wide, bright, toothy smile, topped by a waxed black moustache.

He pirouettes a little with the Trained Nurse against the slow seaweed and the seismic tremolo of the nautch girls—but always with a movement of expectancy, with reiterated turnings and yearnings towards the wings. And at last she comes, radiating ecstasy—the *première danseuse*. Tooth-white, gum-pink, with golden tresses semi-permanently undulating over the spherical false head, whose one feature, the smile, is like a swag of pearls looped up between a pair of dimples—in she floats on toes that barely touch the floor. The music becomes perceptibly more clotted. Prometheus points the way upwards; the philosophy grows profounder in its import.

And now the real action of the ballet begins. Seaweed-armed, seismically stomached, the nautch girls provide the fundamental bass of movement. In front of them, the choreographic drama unfolds itself. It is a theme of pursuit and flight: Pan, Syrinx; Dentist-Apollo and Daphne-Patient. He approaches, high-steppedly gambolling. Timorously she stands, head sideways tilted and downcast, arms close to sides, hands clasped before her. He approaches, approaches, playfully amorous, dancing like a snipe, gambolling like a spider. Every now and then he throws a cart-wheel, dances a few steps on his hands, or jumps, on spring-heeled shoes, six or seven feet into the air. He approaches, he approaches. And though she trembles, though she winces like a colt, though she seems every moment on the point of flying—yet, she holds her ground, lets him come nearer, nearer. Suddenly, from the pocket of his alpaca jacket, he whips out an immense pair of forceps. All the instruments of the band utter a scream; Daphne flies in earnest round the dais and Apollo gambols after. Through the convolutions of their twisted flight and pursuit, the Trained Nurses thrid their way, leaping toreadors of Minos.

Another halt. A variation of the first love-play. Suave gestures with the forceps. The love theme is very prominent in the music. Nearer, nearer. The Dentist's blank face seems to take on an expression of triumph; he is so near, so near; the forceps are raised, open-jawed, towards the swag of pearls. The steel jaws are on the point of closing; but off she goes again, the Dentist following in a dizzy series of *sauts périlleux*. Twice round the central dais. Still he follows. This way and that she flutters; he is always there to cut off her retreat. She runs for protection to the Nurses. But instead of succouring, they receive her on the points of their sharp probes, they drive her back towards the pursuer. Distracted, she flaps from side to side. She sees in front of her the Dentist, blowing kisses with one hand, opening and closing with the other the jaws of his forceps, mockingly reflecting in his pursuit her every velleity of flight to right or left. Behind her the points of six steel prods threaten with imminent puncture. She looks desperately round her; the blank face, the smiling swag of pearls becomes expressive, as the huge round head jerks in panic this way and that, of a lacerating, torturing fear. A loophole of escape seems to present itself. She breaks from between her pursuers, gains in three bounds the summit of the dais and, one hand on the arm of the chair, the other to her heart, stands looking down, momentarily safe. But the safety is only illusory; her position is more than ever hopeless. The Dentist and his Nurses execute a cake-walk in Indian file round the base of the stele on which she has marooned herself. She is trapped beyond the possibility of redemption. The Nurses continue their cake-walk, but the Dentist breaks line and begins to mount the dais, running round and round, spirally, a step higher at every revolution. The Patient gesticulates wildly as he approaches, lifting her blank face, her clawing hands towards heaven. The Dentist reaches the penultimate step. One more revolution, he is on the platform beside her.

He springs forward, embracing her, tries to snatch from the swag of pearls a kiss. She bends backwards, away from his desire, backwards till her head touches her heels. They execute a tango of willowy bendings. The Dentist grows more and more passionate, there is a quickening in the Nurses' cake-walk down below. The Patient begins to yield. She is forced back into the chair. The blank, globed faces come together in a tangential kiss. But even as he kisses, the Dentist reaches up for the Piranesian cable above him, pulls down a formidable drill which revolves as he grasps it. There is a rhythmic and harmonious struggle. The ravished kisses alternate with jabs of the drill, tweaks of the forceps. Resistance grows fainter and fainter, the Dentist more and more surgically amorous. We are at the Coda now; the choir breaks into the music with the supernatural ecstatic note of the human voice.

Resistance is now at an end. The Dentist lifts his yielding Patient from the chair; she droops limply in the crook of his left arm. The rest of the Coda is occupied by the development of a portentous embrace, in which dentistry becomes transcendentally one with passion, and love takes on the character of a surgical operation. The embracement culminates in the inenarrable delights of ecstasy. Ecstasy—the final enormous chord of F sharp major. Shatteringly loud, it bursts upon the ears. Choir, orchestra, steam organ, Parsifal bell instrument, gongs, musical glasses—all sound the chord, keep it held, slowly swelling, minute after minute. And with the flowering of that ecstatic chord the heavens open and God the Father slowly descends over the dais. A swarm of cherubs, whose nacreous flesh seems ready to melt in the intense white limelight, hovers over Him in a domed formation, his living canopy. The chord of F sharp major slowly swells and swells, a long inverted cone of sound. The limelight grows brighter and brighter, God the Father smiles. His velvet draperies float out in the wind of ecstasy. Illumined, the Dentist and his Patient look up, still embraced, still in the throes of a surgical love. And gradually, as the ecstasy grows intenser, as the chord of F sharp major becomes more and more terribly, more sweetly and piercingly loud, gradually they float up from their solid platform, they tread the lime-lit air, they bathe in the divine effulgence. And the trained Nurses—they, too, leave the earth; they, too, yearn upwards in a curved, suspended gesture towards the light. And as the chord increases in volume, as the brazen cone of sound expands and appallingly expands within our grasp—slowly the whole heavenly host, the wriggling canopy of *putti*, the enthroned godhead, the ecstatic mortals float upwards out of sight towards some Higher Sphere.

And suddenly the chord comes to an end; there is the startling silence which follows

the stopping of a mill-wheel. The stage is
quite empty, save for the dado of nautch girls
at the foot of the back wall. They are still
swaying weedily, still tremulously palpitating as the curtain descends.

SIR CHRISTOPHER WREN

THAT an Englishman should be a very great plastic artist is always rather surprising. Perhaps it is a matter of mere chance; perhaps it has something to do with our national character—if such a thing really exists. But, whatever may be the cause, the fact remains that England has produced very few artists of first-class importance. The Renaissance, as it spread, like some marvellous infectious disease of the spirit, across the face of Europe, manifested itself in different countries by different symptoms. In Italy, the country of its origin, the Renaissance was, more than anything, an outburst of painting, architecture and sculpture. Scholarship and religious reformation were, in Germany, the typical manifestations of the disease. But when this gorgeous spiritual measles crossed the English Channel, its symptoms were almost exclusively literary. The first premonitory touch of the infection from Italy "brought out" Chaucer. With the next bout of the disease England produced the Elizabethans. But among all these poets there was not a single plastic artist whose name we so much as remember.

And then, suddenly, the seventeenth century gave birth to two English artists of genius. It produced Inigo Jones and, a little later, Wren. Wren died, at the age of more than ninety, in the spring of 1723. We are celebrating to-day his bi-centenary—celebrating it not merely by antiquarian talk and scholarly appreciations of his style but also (the signs are not wanting) in a more concrete and living way; by taking a renewed interest in the art of which he was so great a master and by reverting in our practice to that fine tradition which he, with his predecessor, Inigo, inaugurated.

An anniversary celebration is an act of what Wordsworth would have called "natural piety"; an act by which past is linked with present, and of the vague, interminable series of the days a single comprehensible and logical unity is created in our minds. At the coming of the centenaries we like to remember the great men of the past, not so much by way of historical exercise, but that we may see precisely where, in relation to their achievement, we stand at the present time, that we may appraise the life still left in their spirit and apply to ourselves the moral of their example. I have no intention in this article of giving a biography of Wren, a list of his works, or a technical account of his style and methods. I propose to do no more than describe, in the most general terms, the nature of his achievement and its significance to ourselves.

Wren was a good architect. But since it is important to know precisely what we are talking about, let us begin by asking ourselves what good architecture is. Descending with majesty from his private Sinai, Mr. Ruskin dictated to a whole generation of Englishmen the aesthetic Law. On monolithic tables that were the Stones of Venice he wrote the great truths that had been revealed to him. Here is one of them:

"It is to be generally observed that the proportions of buildings have nothing to do with the style or general merit of their architecture. An architect trained in the worst schools and utterly devoid of all meaning or purpose in his work, may yet have such a natural gift of massing and grouping as will render his structure effective when seen at a distance."

Now it is to be generally observed, as he himself would say, that in all matters connected with art, Ruskin is to be interpreted as we interpret dreams—that is to say, as signifying precisely the opposite of what he says. Thus, when we find him saying that good architecture has nothing to do with proportion or the judicious disposition of masses, and that the general effect counts for nothing at all, we may take it as more or less definitely proven that good architecture is, in fact, almost entirely a matter of proportion and massing, and that the general effect of the whole work counts for nearly everything. Interpreted according to this simple oneiro-critical method, Ruskin's pontifical pronouncement may be taken as explaining briefly and clearly the secrets of good architecture. That is why I have chosen this quotation to be the text of my discourse on Wren.

For the qualities which most obviously distinguish Wren's work are precisely those which Ruskin so contemptuously disparages and which we, by our process of interpretation, have singled out as the essentially architectural qualities. In all that Wren designed —I am speaking of the works of his maturity; for at the beginning of his career he was still an unpractised amateur, and at the end, though still on occasion wonderfully successful, a very old man—we see a faultless proportion, a felicitous massing and contrasting of forms. He conceived his buildings as three-dimensional designs which should be seen, from every point of view, as harmoniously proportioned wholes. (With regard to the exteriors this, of course, is true only of those buildings which *can* be seen from all sides. Like all true architects, Wren preferred to build in positions where his work could be appreciated three-dimensionally. But he was also a wonderful maker of façades; witness his Middle Temple gateway and his houses in King's Bench Walk.) He possessed in the highest degree that instinctive sense of proportion and scale which enabled him to embody his conception in brick and stone. In his great masterpiece of St. Paul's every part of the building, seen from within or without, seems to stand in a certain satisfying and harmonious relation to every other part. The same is true even of the smallest works belonging to the period of Wren's maturity. On its smaller scale and different plane, such a building as Rochester Guildhall is as beautiful, because as harmonious in the relation of all its parts, as St. Paul's.

Of Wren's other purely architectural qualities I shall speak but briefly. He was, to begin with, an engineer of inexhaustible resource; one who could always be relied upon to find the best possible solution to any problem, from blowing up the ruins of old St. Paul's to providing the new with a dome that should be at once beautiful and thor-

oughly safe.   As a designer he exhibited the
same practical ingenuity.   No architect has
known how to make so much of a difficult
site and cheap materials.   The man who built
the City churches was a practical genius of no
common order.   He was also an artist of profoundly original mind.   This originality reveals itself in the way in which he combines
the accepted features of classical Renaissance
architecture into new designs that were entirely English and his own.   The steeples of
his City churches provide us with an obvious
example of this originality.   His domestic
architecture—that wonderful application of
classical principles to the best in the native
tradition—is another.

But Wren's most characteristic quality—
the quality which gives to his work, over and
above its pure beauty, its own peculiar character and charm—is a quality rather moral
than aesthetic.   Of Chelsea Hospital, Carlyle
once remarked that it was "obviously the
work of a gentleman."   The words are illuminating.   Everything that Wren did was
the work of a gentleman; that is the secret
of its peculiar character.   For Wren was a
great gentleman: one who valued dignity and
restraint and who, respecting himself, re-
spected also humanity; one who desired that
men and women should live with the dignity,

even the grandeur, befitting their proud human title; one who despised meanness and oddity as much as vulgar ostentation; one who admired reason and order, who distrusted all extravagance and excess. A gentleman, the finished product of an old and ordered civilization.

Wren, the restrained and dignified gentleman, stands out most clearly when we compare him with his Italian contemporaries. The baroque artists of the seventeenth century were interested above everything in the new, the startling, the astonishing; they strained after impossible grandeurs, unheard-of violences. The architectural ideals of which they dreamed were more suitable for embodiment in theatrical cardboard than in stone. And indeed, the late seventeenth and early eighteenth century was the golden age of scene-painting in Italy. The artists who painted the settings for the elder Scarlatti's operas, the later Bibienas and Piranesis, came nearer to reaching the wild Italian ideal than ever mere architects like Borromini or Bernini, their imaginations cramped by the stubbornness of stone and the unsleeping activities of gravitations, could hope to do.

How vastly different is the baroque theatricality from Wren's sober restraint!

Wren was a master of the grand style; but he never dreamed of building for effect alone. He was never theatrical or showy, never pretentious or vulgar. St. Paul's is a monument of temperance and chastity. His great palace at Hampton Court is no gaudy stage-setting for the farce of absolute monarchy. It is a country gentleman's house—more spacious, of course, and with statelier rooms and more impressive vistas—but still a house meant to be lived in by some one who was a man as well as a king. But if his palaces might have housed, without the least incongruity, a well-bred gentleman, conversely his common houses were always dignified enough, however small, to be palaces in miniature and the homes of kings.

In the course of the two hundred years which have elapsed since his death, Wren's successors have often departed, with melancholy results, from the tradition of which he was the founder. They have forgotten, in their architecture, the art of being gentlemen. Infected by a touch of the baroque *folie de grandeur*, the architects of the eighteenth century built houses in imitation of Versailles and Caserta—huge stage houses, all for show and magnificence and all but impossible to live in.

The architects of the nineteenth century

sinned in a diametrically opposite way—towards meanness and a negation of art. Senselessly preoccupied with details, they created the nightmare architecture of "features." The sham Gothic of early Victorian times yielded at the end of the century to the nauseous affectation of "sham-peasantry." Big houses were built with all the irregularity and more than the "quaintness" of cottages; suburban villas took the form of machine-made imitations of the Tudor peasant's hut. To all intents and purposes architecture ceased to exist; Ruskin had triumphed.

To-day, however, there are signs that architecture is coming back to that sane and dignified tradition of which Wren was the great exponent. Architects are building houses for gentlemen to live in. Let us hope that they will continue to do so. There may be sublimer types of men than the gentleman: there are saints, for example, and the great enthusiasts whose thoughts and actions move the world. But for practical purposes and in a civilized, orderly society, the gentleman remains, after all, the ideal man. The most profound religious emotions have been expressed in Gothic architecture. Human ambitions and aspirations have been most colossally reflected by the Romans and the Italians of the baroque. But it is in England that the golden mean of reasonableness and decency—the practical philosophy of the civilized man—has received its most elegant and dignified expression. The old gentleman who died two hundred years ago preached on the subject of civilization a number of sermons in stone. St. Paul's and Greenwich, Trinity Library and Hampton Court, Chelsea, Kilmainham, Blackheath and Rochester, St. Stephen's Walbrook and St. Mary Ab-church, Kensington orangery and Middle Temple gateway—these are the titles of a few of them. They have much, if we will study them, to teach us.

THE COUNTRY

IT is a curious fact, of which I can think of no satisfactory explanation, that enthusiasm for country life and love of natural scenery are strongest and most widely diffused precisely in those European countries which have the worst climate and where the search for the picturesque involves the greatest discomfort. Nature worship increases in an exact ratio with distance from the Mediterranean. The Italians and the Spanish have next to no interest in nature for its own sake. The French feel a certain affection for the country, but not enough to make them desire to live in it if they can possibly inhabit the town. The South Germans and Swiss form an apparent exception to the rule. They live nearer to the Mediterranean than the Parisians, and yet they are fonder of the country. But the exception, as I have said, is only apparent; for, owing to their remoteness from the ocean and the mountainous conformation of the land, these people enjoy for a large part of each year a climate that is, to all intents, arctic. In England, where the climate is detestable, we love the country so much that we are prepared, for the privilege of living in it, to get up at seven, summer and winter, bicycle, wet or fine, to a distant station and make an hour's journey to our place of labour. In our spare moments we go for walking tours, and we regard caravanning as a pleasure. In Holland the climate is far more unpleasant than in England, and we should consequently expect the Dutch to be even keener country-fanciers than ourselves. The ubiquitous water makes it difficult, however, for season-ticket holders to settle down casually in the Dutch countryside. But if unsuitable as building land, the soggy meadows of the Low Countries are firm enough to carry tents. Unable to live permanently in the country, the Dutch are the greatest campers in the world. Poor Uncle Toby, when he was campaigning in those parts, found the damp so penetrating that he was forced to burn good brandy in his tent to dry the air. But then my Uncle Toby was a mere Englishman, brought up in a climate which, compared with that of Holland, is balmy. The hardier Dutch camp out for pleasure. Of northern Germany it is enough to say that it is the home of the wander-birds. And as for Scandinavia—it is well known that there is no part of the world, excluding the tropics, where people so freely divest themselves of their clothing. The Swedish passion for nature is so strong that it can only be adequately expressed when in a state of nature. "As souls unbodied," says Donne, "bodies unclothed must be to taste whole joys." Noble, nude, and far more modern than any other people in Europe, they sport in the icy waters of the Baltic, they roam naked in the primeval forest. The cautious Italian, meanwhile, bathes in his tepid sea during only two months out of the twelve; always wears a vest under his shirt, and never leaves the town, if he can possibly help it, except when the summer is at its most hellish, and again, for a little while, in the autumn, to superintend the making of his wine.

Strange and inexplicable state of affairs! Is it that the dwellers under inclement skies are trying to bluff themselves into a belief that they inhabit Eden? Do they deliberately love nature in the hope of persuading themselves that she is as beautiful in the damp and darkness as in the sunlight? Do they brave the discomforts of northern country life in order to be able to say to those who live in more favoured lands: You see, our countryside is just as delightful as yours; and the proof is that we live in it!

But whatever the reason, the fact remains that nature worship does increase with distance from the sun. To search for causes is hopeless; but it is easy and at the same time not uninteresting to catalogue effects. Thus, our Anglo-Saxon passion for the country has had the result of turning the country into one vast town; but a town without the urban conveniences which makes tolerable life in a city. For we all love the country so much that we desire to live in it, if only during the night, when we are not at work. We build cottages, buy season tickets and bicycles to take us to the station. And meanwhile the country perishes. The Surrey I know as a boy was full of wildernesses. To-day Hindhead is hardly distinguishable from the Elephant and Castle. Mr. Lloyd George has built a week-end cottage (not, one feels, without a certain appositeness) at the foot of the Devil's Jumps; and several thousand people are busily following his example. Every lane is now a street. Harrod's and Selfridge's call daily. There is no more country, at any rate within fifty miles of London. Our love has killed it.

Except in summer, when it is too hot to stay in town, the French, and still more, the Italians, do not like the country. The result is that they still have country not to like. Solitude stretches almost to the gates of Paris. (And Paris, remember, still has gates;

you drive up to them along country roads, enter and find yourself within a few minutes of the centre of the city.)   The silence sleeps unbroken, except by the faint music of ghosts, within a mile of the Victor Emanuel monument at Rome.

In France, in Italy none but countrymen live in the country.   Agriculture there is taken seriously; farms are still farms and not week-end cottages; and the corn is still permitted to grow on what, in England, would be desirable building land.

In Italy, despite the fact that the educated Italians like the country still less than the French, there are fewer complete solitudes than in France, because there are more countrymen.   And how few there are in France! A drive from the Belgian frontier to the Mediterranean puts life and meaning into those statistics from which we learn, academically and in theory, that France is under-populated.   Long stretches of open road extend between town and town.

> Like stones of worth they thinly placed are,
> Or captain jewels in the carcanet.

Even the villages are few and far between. And those innumerable farms which shine out from among the olive trees on Italian hillsides—one looks in vain for their French counterpart. Driving through the fertile plains of Central France, one can turn one's eyes over the fields and scarcely see a house. And then, what forests still grown on French soil! Huge tracts of uninhabited woodland, with not a week-ender or a walking-tourist to be seen within their shades.

This state of things is delightful to me personally; for I like the country, enjoy solitude, and take no interest in the political future of France. But to a French patriot I can imagine that a drive across his native land must seem depressing. Huge populations, upon whose skulls the bump of philoprogenitiveness can be seen at a quarter of a mile, pullulate on the farther side of almost every frontier. Without haste, without rest, as though by a steadily continued miracle, the Germans and the Italians multiply themselves, like loaves and fishes. Every three years a million brand-new Teutons peer across the Rhine, a million Italians are wondering where they are going to find room, in their narrow country, to live. And there are no more Frenchmen. Twenty years hence, what will happen? The French Government offers prizes to those who produce large families. In vain; everybody knows all about birth control, and even in the least educated classes there are no prejudices and

a great deal of thrift.   Hordes of blacka-
moors are drilled and armed; but blacka-
moors can be but a poor defence, in the long
run, against European philoprogenitiveness.
Sooner or later, this half-empty land will be
colonized.   It may be done peacefully, it
may be done with violence; let us hope peacefully, with the consent and at the invitation
of the French themselves.   Already the
French import, temporarily, I forget how
many foreign labourers every year.   In time,
no doubt, the foreigners will begin to settle:
the Italians in the south, the Germans in the
east, the Belgians in the north, perhaps even
a few English in the west.

Frenchmen may not like the plan; but
until all nations agree to practise birth control to exactly the same extent, it is the best
that can be devised.

The Portuguese who, in the later sixteenth
and the seventeenth century, suffered acutely
from under-population (half the able-bodied
men had emigrated to the colonies, where
they died in war or of tropical diseases, while
those who stayed at home were periodically
decimated by famine—for the colonies produced only gold, not bread) solved their
problem by importing negro slaves to work
the deserted fields.   The negroes settled.
They intermarried with the inhabitants.   In

two or three generations the race which had conquered half the world was extinct, and Portugal, with the exception of a small area in the north, was inhabited by a hybrid race of Eur-Africans. The French may think themselves lucky if, avoiding war, they can fill their depleted country with civilized white men.

Meanwhile, the emptiness of France is a delight to every lover of nature and solitude. But even in Italy, where farms and peasants and peasants' children are thick on the land, the lover of the country feels much happier than he does in what may actually be more sparsely inhabited districts of the home counties. For farms and peasants are country products, as truly native to the land as trees or growing corn, and as inoffensive. It is the urban interloper who ruins the English country. Neither he nor his house belong to it. In Italy, on the other hand, when the rare trespasser from the town does venture into the country, he finds it genuinely rustic. The country is densely populated, but it is still the country. It has not been killed by the deadly kindness of those who, like myself, are nature's townsmen.

The time is not far distant, I am afraid, when every countryside in Europe, even the Spanish, will be invaded by nature lovers from the towns. It is not so long ago, after all, since Evelyn was horrified and disgusted by the spectacle of the rocks at Clifton. Till the end of the eighteenth century every sensible man, even in England, even in Sweden, feared and detested mountains. The modern enthusiasm for wild nature is a recent growth and began—along with kindness to animals, industrialism and railway travelling —among the English. (It is, perhaps, not surprising that the people who first made their cities uninhabitable with dirt, noise and smoke should also have been the first to love nature.) From this island country sentiment has spread with machinery. All the world welcomed machinery with delight; but country sentiment has so far flourished only in the north. Still, there are evident signs that even the Latins are becoming infected by it. In France and Italy wild nature has become —though to a far less extent than in England—the object of *snobisme*. It is rather chic, in those countries, to be fond of nature. In a few years, I repeat, everybody will adore it as a matter of course. For even in the north those who do not in the least like the country are made to imagine that they do by the artful and never-ceasing suggestions of the people whose interest it is that the country should be liked. No modern man, even if he loathed the country, could resist the appeal of the innumerable advertisements, published by railways, motor car manufacturers, thermos flask makers, sporting tailors, house agents and all the rest whose livelihood depends on his frequently visiting the country. Now the art of advertising is still poorly developed in the Latin countries. But it is improving even there. The march of progress is irresistible. Fiat and the State Railways have only to hire American advertising managers to turn the Italians into a race of week-enders, and season-ticket holders. Already there is a *Città Giardino* on the outskirts of Rome; Ostia is being developed as a residential seaside suburb; the recently opened motor road has placed the Lakes at the mercy of Milan. My grandchildren, I foresee, will have to take their holidays in Central Asia.

ON DEVIATING INTO SENSE

THERE is a story, very dear for some reason to our ancestors, that Apelles, or I forget what other Greek painter, grown desperate at the failure of his efforts to portray realistically the foam on a dog's mouth, threw his sponge at the picture in a pet, and was rewarded for his ill-temper by discovering that the resultant smudge was the living image of the froth whose aspect he had been unable, with all his art, to recapture. No one will ever know the history of all the happy mistakes, the accidents and unconscious deviations into genius, that have helped to enrich the world's art. They are probably countless. I myself have deviated more than once into accidental felicities. Recently, for example, the hazards of careless typewriting caused me to invent a new portmanteau word of the most brilliantly Laforguian quality. I had meant to write the phrase "the Human Comedy," but, by a happy slip, I put my finger on the letter that stands next to "C" on the universal keyboard. When I came to read over the completed page I found that I had written "the Human Vomedy." Was there ever a criti-

cism of life more succinct and expressive?
To the more sensitive and queasy among the
gods the last few years must indeed have
seemed a vomedy of the first order.

The grossest forms of mistake have played
quite a distinguished part in the history of
letters. One thinks, for example, of the
name Criseida or Cressida manufactured out
of a Greek accusative, of that Spenserian
misunderstanding of Chaucer which gave cur-
rency to the rather ridiculous substantive
"derring-do." Less familiar, but more deliciously absurd, is Chaucer's slip in reading
"naves ballatrices" for "naves bellatrices"—
Ballet-ships instead of battle-ships—and his
translation "shippes hoppesteres." But these
broad, straightforward howlers are uninteresting compared with the more subtle deviations into originality occasionally achieved
by authors who were trying their best not to
be original. Nowhere do we find more remarkable examples of accidental brilliance
than among the post-Chaucerian poets, whose
very indistinct knowledge of what precisely
was the metre in which they were trying to
write often caused them to produce very
striking variations on the staple English
measure.

Chaucer's variations from the decasyllable
norm were deliberate. So, for the most part,

were those of his disciple Lydgate, whose favourite "broken-backed" line, lacking the first syllable of the iambus that follows the caesura, is metrically of the greatest interest to contemporary poets. Lydgate's characteristic line follows this model:

For speechéless nothing maist thou speed.

Judiciously employed, the broken-backed line might yield very beautiful effects. Lydgate, as has been said, was probably pretty conscious of what he was doing. But his procrustean methods were apt to be a little indiscriminate, and one wonders sometimes whether he was playing variations on a known theme or whether he was rather tentatively groping after the beautiful regularity of his master Chaucer. The later fifteenth and sixteenth century poets seem to have worked very much in the dark. The poems of such writers as Hawes and Skelton abound in the vaguest parodies of the decasyllable line. Anything from seven to fifteen syllables will serve their turn. With them the variations are seldom interesting. Chance had not much opportunity of producing subtle metrical effects with a man like Skelton, whose mind was naturally so full of jigging doggerel that his variations on the decasyllable are mostly in the nature of

rough skeltonics.   I have found interesting
accidental variations on the decasyllable in
Heywood, the writer of moralities.   This,
from the *Play of Love*, has a real metrical
beauty:

Felt ye but one pang such as I feel many,
One pang of despair or one pang of desire,
One pang of one displeasant look of her eye,
One pang of one word of her mouth as in ire,
Or in restraint of her love which I desire—
One pang of all these, felt once in all your life,
Should quail your opinion and quench all our strife.

These dactylic resolutions of the third and
fourth lines are extremely interesting.

But the most remarkable example of accidental metrical invention that I have yet
come across is to be found in the Earl of
Surrey's translation of Horace's ode on the
golden mean.   Surrey was one of the pio-
neers of the reaction against the vagueness
and uncertain carelessness of the post-
Chaucerians.   From the example of Italian
poetry he had learned that a line must have
a fixed number of syllables.   In all his poems
his aim is always to achieve regularity at
whatever cost.   To make sure of having ten
syllables in every line it is evident that
Surrey made use of his fingers as well as his
ears.   We see him at his worst and most

laborious in the first stanza of his translation:

> Of thy life, Thomas, this compass well mark:
> Not aye with full sails the high seas to beat;
> Ne by coward dread in shunning storms dark
> On shallow shores thy keel in peril freat.

The ten syllables are there all right, but except in the last line there is no recognizable rhythm of any kind, whether regular or irregular.   But when Surrey comes to the second stanza—

> Auream quisquis mediocritatem
> Diligit, tutus caret obsoleti
> Sordibus tecti, caret invidenda
> Sobrius aula—

some lucky accident inspires him with the genius to translate in these words:

> Whoso gladly halseth the golden mean,
> Void of dangers advisedly hath his home;
> Not with loathsome muck as a den unclean,
> Nor palace like, whereat disdain may gloam.

Not only is this a very good translation, but it is also a very interesting and subtle metrical experiment.   What could be more felicitous than this stanza made up of three trochaic lines, quickened by beautiful dactylic resolutions, and a final iambic line of regular measure—the recognized tonic chord that brings the music to its close?   And yet the tunelessness of the first stanza is enough to prove that Surrey's achievement is as much a product of accident as the foam on the jaws of Apelles' dog.   He was doing his best all the time to write decasyllables with the normal iambic beat of the last line.   His failures to do so were sometimes unconscious strokes of genius.

SABBIONETA

"THEY call it the Palazzo del Te," said the maid at the little inn in the back street where we had lunch, "because the Gonzaga used to go and take tea there." And that was all that she, and probably most of the other inhabitants of Mantua, knew about the Gonzaga or their palaces. It was surprising, perhaps, that she should have known so much. Gonzaga—the name, at least, still faintly reverberated. After two hundred years, how many names are still remembered? Few indeed. The Gonzaga, it seemed to me, enjoy a degree of immortality that might be envied them. They have vanished, they are as wholly extinct as the dinosaur; but in the cities they once ruled their name still vaguely echoes, and for those who care to listen they have left behind some of the most eloquent sermons on the vanity of human wishes and the mutability of fortune that stones have ever mutely preached.

I have seen many ruins and of every period. Stonehenge and Ansedonia, Ostia and mediaeval Ninfa (which the Duke of Sermoneta is busily turning into the likeness of a neat suburban park), Bolsover and the

gruesome modern ruins in northern France.
I have seen great cities dead or in decay:
Pisa, Bruges and the newly murdered Vienna.
But over none, it seemed to me, did there
brood so profound a melancholy as over
Mantua; none seemed so dead or so utterly
bereft of glory; nowhere was desolation more
pregnant with the memory of splendour, the
silence nowhere so richly musical with echoes.
There are a thousand rooms in the labyrinthine Reggia at Mantua—Gothic rooms,
rooms of the Renaissance, baroque rooms,
rooms rich with the absurd pretentious decorations of the First Empire, huge presence
chambers and closets and the horribly exquisite apartments of the dwarfs—a thousand rooms, and their walls enclose an emptiness that is the mournful ghost of departed
plenitude. It is through Mallarmé's *creux
néant musicien* that one walks in Mantua.

And not in Mantua alone. For wherever
the Gonzaga lived, they left behind them the
same pathetic emptiness, the same pregnant
desolation, the same echoes, the same ghosts
of splendour.

The Palazzo del Te is made sad and beautiful with the same melancholy as broods in
the Reggia. True, the stupid vulgarity of
Giulio Romano was permitted to sprawl
over its walls in a series of deplorable fres-

coes (it is curious, by the way, that Giulio
Romano should have been the only Italian
artist of whom Shakespeare had ever heard,
or at least the only one he ever mentioned);
but the absurdities and grossnesses seem actually to make the place more touching. The
departed tenants of the palace become in a
manner more real to one, when one discovers
that their taste ran to *trompe l'œil* pictures
of fighting giants and mildly pornographic
scenes out of pagan mythology. And seem-
ing more human, they seem also more dead;
and the void left by their disappearance is
more than ever musical with sadness.

Even the cadets of the Gonzaga house enjoyed a power of leaving behind them a more
than Pompeian desolation. Twenty miles
from Mantua, on the way to Cremona, is a
village called Sabbioneta. It lies near the
Po, though not on its banks; possesses, for a
village, a tolerably large population, mostly
engaged in husbandry; is rather dirty and has
an appearance—probably quite deceptive—
of poverty. In fact it is just like all other
villages of the Lombard plain, but with this
difference: a Gonzaga once lived here. The
squalor of Sabbioneta is no common squalor;
it is a squalor that was once magnificence.
Its farmers and horse-copers live, dirtily and
destructively, in treasures of late Renais-

sance architecture. The town hall is a ducal
palace; in the municipal school, children are
taught under carved and painted ceilings, and
when the master is out of the room they write
their names on the marble bellies of the patient, battered caryatids who uphold the
scutcheoned mantel. The weekly cinema
show is given in an Olympic theatre, built a
few years after the famous theatre at Vicenza, by Palladio's pupil, Scamozzi. The
people worship in sumptuous churches, and if
ever soldiers happen to pass through the
town, they are billeted in the deserted summer palace.

The creator of all these splendours was
Vespasiano, son of that Luigi Gonzaga,
the boon companion of kings, whom, for his
valour and his fabulous strength, his contemporaries nicknamed Rodomonte. Luigi
died young, killed in battle, and his son Vespasiano was brought up by his aunt, Giulia
Gonzaga, one of the most perfectly courtly
ladies of her age. She had him taught Latin,
Greek, the mathematics, good manners and
the art of war. This last he practised with
distinction, serving at one time or another
under many princes, but chiefly under
Philip II. of Spain, who honoured him with
singular favours. Vespasiano seems to have
been the typical Italian tyrant of his period

—cultured, intelligent, and only just so much of an ungovernably ferocious ruffian as one would expect a man to be who has been brought up in the possession of absolute power. It was in the intimacy of private life that he displayed his least amiable characteristics. He poisoned his first wife on a suspicion, probably unfounded, of her infidelity, murdered her supposed lover and exiled his relations. His second wife left him mysteriously after three years of married life and died of pure misery in a convent, carrying with her into the grave nobody knew what frightful secret. His third wife, it is true, lived to a ripe old age; but then Vespasiano himself died after only a few years of marriage. His only son, whom he loved with the anxious passion of the ambitious parvenu who desires to found a dynasty, one day annoyed him by not taking off his cap when he met him in the street. Vespasiano rebuked him for this lack of respect. The boy answered back impertinently. Whereupon Vespasiano gave him such a frightful kick in the groin that the boy died. Which shows that, even when chastising one's own children, it is advisable to observe the Queensberry rules.

It was in 1560 that Vespasiano decided to convert the miserable village from which he took his title into a capital worthy of its ruler. He set to work with energy. In a few years the village of squalid cottages clustering round a feudal castle had given place to a walled town, with broad streets, two fine squares, a couple of palaces and a noble Gallery of Antiques. These last Vespasiano had inherited from his father, Rodomonte, who had been at the sack of Rome in 1527 and had shown himself an industrious and discriminating looter. Sabbioneta was in its turn looted by the Austrians, who carried off Rodomonte's spoils to Mantua. The museum remains; but there is nothing in it but the *creux néant musicien* which the Gonzaga alone, of all the princes in Italy, had the special art of creating by their departure.

We had come to Sabbioneta from Parma. In the vast Farnese palace there is no musically echoing void—merely an ordinary, undisturbing emptiness. Only in the colossal Farnesian theatre does one recapture anything like the Mantuan melancholy. We drove through Colorno, where the last of the Farnesi built a summer palace about as large as Hampton Court. Over the Po, by a bridge of boats, through Casalmaggiore and on, tortuously, by little by-roads across the plain. A line of walls presented themselves, a handsome gate. We drove in, and immediately faint ghostly oboes began to play around us; we were in Sabbioneta among the Gonzaga ghosts.

The central piazza of the town is oblong; Vespasiano's palace stands at one of the shorter ends, presenting to the world a modest façade, five windows wide, once rich with decorations, but now bare. It serves at present as town hall. In the waiting-room on the first floor stand four life-sized equestrian figures, carved in wood and painted, representing four of Vespasiano's ancestors. Once there was a squadron of twelve; but the rest have been broken up and burned. This crime, together with all the other ravages committed by time or vandals in the course of three centuries, was attributed by the mayor, who personally did us the honours of his municipality, to the Socialists who had preceded him in office. It is unnecessary to add that he himself was a Fascista.

We walked round in the emptiness under the superbly carved and gilded ceilings. The porter sat among decayed frescoes in the Cabinet of Diana. The town council held its meetings in the Ducal Saloon. The Gallery of the Ancestors housed a clerk and the municipal archives. The deputy mayor had his

office in the Hall of the Elephants. The
Sala d'Oro had been turned into an infants'
class-room. We walked out again into the
sunlight fairly heart-broken.

The Olympic Theatre is a few yards down
the street. Accompanied by the obliging
young porter from the Cabinet of Diana,
we entered. It is a tiny theatre, but complete and marvellously elegant. From the
pit, five semicircular steps rise to a pillared
loggia, behind which—having the width of
the whole auditorium—is the ducal box.
The loggia consists of twelve Corinthian
pillars, topped by a cornice. On the cornice,
above each pillar, stand a dozen stucco gods
and goddesses. Noses and fingers, paps and
ears have gone the way of all art; but the
general form of them survives. Their white
silhouettes gesticulate elegantly against the
twilight of the hall.

The stage was once adorned with a fixed
scene in perspective, like that which Palladio
built at Vicenza. The mayor wanted us to
believe that it was his Bolshevik predecessors
who had destroyed it; but as a matter of fact
it was taken down about a century ago.
Gone, too, are the frescoes with which the
walls were once covered. One year of epi-
demic the theatre was used as a fever hos-

pital. When the plague had passed, it was thought that the frescoes needed disinfecting; they were thickly whitewashed. There is no money to scrape the whitewash off again.

We followed the young porter out of the theatre. Another two or three hundred yards and we were in the Piazza d'Armi. It is an oblong, grassy space. On the long axis of the rectangle, near one end there stands, handsomely pedestalled, a fluted marble column, topped by a statue of Athena, the tutelary goddess of Vespasiano's metropolis. The pedestal, the capital and the statue are of the late Renaissance. But the column is antique, and formed a part of Rodomonte's Roman booty. Rodomonte was evidently no petty thief. If a thing is worth doing it is worth doing thoroughly; that, evidently, was his motto.

One of the long sides of the rectangle is occupied by the Gallery of Antiques. It is a superb building, architecturally by far the finest thing in the town. The lower storey consists of an open arcade, and the walls of the gallery above are ornamented with blind arches, having well-proportioned windows at the centre of each and separated from one another by Tuscan pilasters. A very bold projecting cornice, topped by a low roof, finishes the design, which for sober and massive elegance is one of the most remarkable of its kind with which I am acquainted.

The opposite side of the piazza is open, a hedge separating it from the back gardens of the neighbouring houses. It was here, I fancy, that the feudal castle originally stood. It was pulled down, however, during the eighteenth century (busy Bolsheviks!) and its bricks employed, more usefully but less aesthetically, to strengthen the dykes which defend the surrounding plain, none too impregnably, from the waters of the Po.

Its destruction has left Vespasiano's summer palace, or Palace of the Garden, isolated (save where it joins the Gallery of the Antiques), and rather forlorn at the end of the long piazza. It is a long, low building of only two storeys, rather insignificant from outside. It is evident that Vespasiano built it as economically as he could. For him the place was only a week-end cottage, a holiday resort, whither he could escape from the metropolitan splendour and bustle of the palace in the market-place, a quarter of a mile away. Like all other rulers of small states, Vespasiano must have found it extremely difficult to take an effective holiday. He could not go ten miles in any direction without coming to a frontier. Within his dominions it was impossible to have a change of air. Wisely, therefore, he decided to concentrate his magnificences. He built his Balmoral within five minutes' walk of his Buckingham Palace.

We knocked at the door. The caretaker who opened to us was an old woman who might have gone on to any stage and acted Juliet's Nurse without a moment's rehearsal. Within the first two minutes of our acquaintance with her she confided to us that she had just got married—for the third time, at the age of seventy. Her comments on the connubial state were so very Juliet's Nurse, so positively Wife-of-Bath, that we were made to feel quite early Victorian in comparison with this robustious old gammer from the *quattrocento*. After having told us all that can be told (and much that cannot be told, at any rate in polite society) about the married state, she proceeded to do us the honours of the house. She led the way, opening the shutters of each room in the long suite as we entered it. And as the light came in through the unglazed windows, what Gonzagesque ravishments were revealed to us! There was a Cabinet of Venus, with the remains of voluptuous nudes; a Hall of the Winds, with puffing cherubs and a mantel in red marble; a Cabinet of the Caesars, floored with

marble and adorned with medallions of all
the ruffians of antiquity; a Hall of the
Myths, on whose ceiling, vaulted into the
likeness of a truncated pyramid seen from
within, were five delightful scenes from Lem-
prière—an Icarus, an Apollo and Marsyas, a
Phaeton, an Arachne and, in the midst, a to
me somewhat mysterious scene: a naked
beauty sitting on the back, not of a bull (that
would have been simple enough), but of a
reclining horse, which turns its head amor-
ously towards her, while she caresses its neck.
Who was the lady and who the travestied
god I do not rightly know. Vague memories
of an escapade of Saturn's float through my
mind. But perhaps I am slandering a respectable deity.

But in any case, whatever its subject, the
picture is charming. Vespasiano's principal
artist was Bernardino Campi of Cremona.
He was not a good painter, of course; but at
least he was gracefully and charmingly, instead of vulgarly, mediocre, like Giulio
Romano. About the Palazzo del Te there
hangs a certain faded frightfulness; but the
Giardino is all sweetness—mannered, no
doubt, and rather feeble—but none the less
authentic in its ruinous decay.

The old caretaker expounded the pictures
to us as we went round—not out of any

knowledge of what they represented, but purely out of her imagination, which was a good deal more interesting. In the Hall of the Graces, where the walls are adorned with what remains of a series of very pretty little *grotteschi* in the Pompeian manner, her fancy surpassed itself. These, she said, were the records of the Duke's dreams. Each time he dreamed a dream he sent for his painter and had it drawn on the walls of this room. These—she pointed to a pair of Chimaeras —he saw in a nightmare; these dancing satyrs visited his sleep after a merry evening; these four urns were dreamt of after too much wine. As for the three naked Graces, from whom the room takes its name, as for those—over the Graces she once more became too Wife-of-Bath to be recorded.

Her old cracked laughter went echoing down the empty rooms; and it seemed to precipitate and crystallize all the melancholy suspended, as it were, in solution within those bleared and peeling walls. The sense of desolation, vaguely felt before, became poignant. And when the old woman ushered us into another room, dark and smelling of mould like the rest, and threw open the shutters and called what the light revealed the "Hall of the Mirrors," I could almost have wept. For in the Hall of the

Mirrors there are no more mirrors, only the elaborate framing of them on walls and ceiling. Where the glasses of Murano once shone are spaces of bare plaster that stare out like blind eyes, blankly and, it seems after a little, reproachfully. "They used to dance in this room," said the old woman.

WHERE ARE THE MOVIES
MOVING?

IN the course of one of his adventures, my favourite dramatic hero, Felix the Cat, begins to sing. He thrums his guitar, he rolls up his eyes, he opens his mouth. A stream of crotchets and semi-quavers comes gushing out of his throat; the little black notes hang in the air above him. Looking up, Felix sees them suspended there. With his usual resourcefulness he realizes at once that these crotchets are exactly the things he has been looking for. He reaches up, catches a few handfuls of them, and before you can say knife he has fitted them together into the most ingenious little trolley or scooter, of which the wheels are made out of the round heads of the notes, the framework of their tails. He helps his companion into her seat, climbs in himself, seizes by its barbs the semi-quaver which serves as the lever of propulsion and, working it vigorously backwards and forwards, shoots out of the picture towards some unknown region of bliss to which we are not privileged to follow him.

Seen on the screen, this conversion of song into scooters seems the most natural and logical thing in the world. The cat opens his mouth; notes, the written symbols of sound, appear in the air above him. Put aside their symbolical significance and concentrate only on their shape; the notes are circles attached to lines—wheels and rods, the raw material of the engineer. Out of these wheels and rods, Felix, cat of all trades, makes a scooter. There is no improbability, no flaw in the artistic logic. One image easily and naturally suggests the other. For the dramatist of the screen, this sort of thing is child's play.

As a mere word-monger and literary man, I envy him. For if I tried to do the same thing in terms of words, the result would be very nearly nonsense. I might write like this, for example: "Don Juan touched his guitar and began to sing *Deh, vieni alla finestra*. The notes floated out and hung in the soft warm air of the Spanish night like the component parts of a Ford car waiting to be assembled." At a first reading, this simile would seem quite incomprehensible, not to say deliberately idiotic. Prolonged reflection might at last extract from the phrase its meaning; the resemblance between printed notes and the parts of a motorcar might finally suggest itself to the imagination. But the process would certainly be slow, and, being slow, would be unsatisfactory. A simile that is understood with difficulty is a bad simile. In a good simile or striking metaphor the two terms, however remote from one another, must be made to come together, so to speak, with a smart click in the reader's mind. To the average mind the connection between notes and spare parts is not immediately obvious. (To begin with, the idea suggested by the words "notes" or "song" is primarily an idea of sound; it is only on second thoughts that one recalls the printed symbol.) Hence the inadequacy and ineffectiveness of the simile, when expressed in words. On the screen, where it is expressed in images, it is perfectly satisfactory.

I have dwelt at some length on Felix's song and scooter—but not, I think, unduly. For the example indicates very clearly what are the most pregnant potentialities of the cinema; it shows how cinematography differs from literature and drama and how it may be developed into something entirely novel. What the cinema can do better than literature or the spoken drama is to be fantastic.

An artist who uses words as his medium finds himself severely limited in the expression of fantasy by the fact that the words he uses are not his own invention, but traditional and hereditary things, impregnated by centuries of use with definite meanings and associations. To a certain extent a writer must employ clichés in order to be understood at all; he cannot dissociate long united ideas, nor bring together ideas that have never been previously joined, without appearing to his readers to be writing nonsense. We have seen, for example, how difficult it would be for a writer to associate in a single phrase the ideas of musical notes and the parts of a motor-car,—and how easy for the maker of films who can almost arbitrarily associate any two ideas, simply by bringing together a pair of suitable images. "Young" writers, especially in France, have for some years past been in rebellion against the tyrannies of language. They have tried forcibly to dissociate anciently joined ideas, to use words in an entirely new way. It cannot be said that the results have been very successful. To the general public their writing seems nonsensical; and even their admirers find that their books make difficult reading. The fact is that these young writers are rebelling, not against old conventions, but against language itself. They are trying to make words do what they cannot do; they are working in the wrong medium. You cannot do silversmith's work in terms of Egyptian granite. Similarly, the most extravagant flights of fancy cannot be rendered in words; on the screen, however, it is easy to give them form. "Super-realism" is the latest of these young French schools. The aim of the super-realists is to free literature completely from logic and to give it the quality of dreams. What they attempt to do, quite unsuccessfully, the cinema achieves brilliantly. The adventures of Felix the Cat are super-realistic in the highest degree.

And not only Felix.

Many of our best films are super-realist or dream-like in character. For example, those hilarious nightmares of Charlie Chaplin and the adventure films of Douglas Fairbanks. In future, I am sure, the tendency will be to exploit this potentiality of the cinema to an ever-increasing extent. It is inevitable; the medium lends itself so well to "super-realism" that it would be extraordinary if this were not to be the case. On the screen miracles are easily performed, the most incongruous ideas can be arbitrarily associated, the limitations of time and space can be largely ignored. Moreover, the very imperfections of the cinema are, in this respect, an enormous asset. The absence of colour is already a bold and arbitrary simplification of reality. The silence in which even the most violent action takes place is wonderfully nightmarish. How strangely fantastic it is to look on at some furious fight in which mortal blows are soundlessly given and received! It is like watching a battle of fishes through the glass of an aquarium.

And then the darkness of the theatre, the monotonous music, inducing, as they do, a kind of hypnotic state, enhance in the minds of the spectators the dream-like quality of what they see on the screen.

In future, then, the "super-realistic" potentialities of the cinema will be more deliberately exploited than they are now. This does not mean, of course, that ordinary realism will be ousted from the screen. It does not mean that all films will come in time to be as wildly fantastic as the exploits of Felix, or even as those of Charlie Chaplin. The cinema will continue to unfold its everyday epics. Realism will persist side by side with super-realism—but a little leavened by it, let us hope, and a little enlivened by its efforts to compete with it.

Broadly speaking, there are two ways in which a story may be told on the screen. The first method is what I may call the Behaviourist method. The story is told in terms of psychological details. The film abounds in significant close-ups of faces, hands, feet moving under the stress of emotion. The method is an excellent one provided that the actors know how to act. Practised by mediocre producers and players, it leads to the most horribly dreary results. The second method, which is favoured especially by the Germans and, more recently, by the Italians, may be called the Symbolical, Expressionist or Pictorial method. For the practitioners of this school the small psychological details of behaviour under emotional stress are not so important as the general pictorial effect of the scene regarded as an expressive symbol. Where the behaviourists would present a close-up of a face gone suddenly rigid, a nervously twitching hand, the expressionists build up a more or less fantastic scenic picture, the general effect of which is expressive of horror, or whatever the emotion to be rendered may be. The great defect of this expressionism has consisted, so far, in its pretentiousness and humourlessness. Touched with a lighter fancy, it might be used very much more successfully than it is. A study of Felix the Cat would teach the Germans some valuable lessons. My own hope and belief is that the behaviourist school of producers will borrow hints from the expressionists, will touch their prosaic realism with a certain picturesque super-realism. Those dismal stories of millionaires, heavy fathers, villains, adultery and so forth would be made more lively by being treated in a less solemn and ponderously direct manner.

CONXOLUS

TO know what everybody else knows—
that Virgil, for example, wrote the
Aeneid, or that the sum of the angles of a
triangle is equal to two right angles—is
rather boring and undistinguished. If you
want to acquire a reputation for learning at
a cheap rate, it is best to ignore the dull and
stupid knowledge which is everybody's possession and concentrate on something odd
and out of the way. Instead of quoting
Virgil quote Sidonius Apollinaris, and express loudly your contempt of those who prefer the court poet of Augustus to the pane-
gyrist of Avitus, Majorianus and Anthemius.
When the conversation turns on *Jane Eyre*
or *Wuthering Heights* (which of course you
have not read) say you infinitely prefer *The
Tenant of Wildfell Hall*. When Donne is
praised, pooh-pooh him and tell the praiser
that he should read Gongora. At the mention of Raphael, make as though to vomit
outright (though you have never been inside
the Vatican); the Raphael Mengses at
Petersburg, you will say, are the only tolerable paintings. In this way you will get
the reputation of a person of profound learn-

ing and the most exquisite taste. Whereas, if you give proof of knowing your Dickens, of having read the Bible, the English classics, Euclid and Horace, nobody will think anything of you at all. You will be just like everybody else.

The extreme inadequacy of my education has often led me, in the course of my journalistic career, to adopt these tactics. I have written airily of the remote and odd in order to conceal my ignorance of the near and the classical. The profession of a literary journalist is not one that greatly encourages honesty. Everything conspires to make him a charlatan. He has no leisure to read regularly or with purpose; at the same time reviewing makes him acquainted with a mass of fragmentary and miscellaneous information. He would be a prodigy of intellectual integrity if he did not reproduce it in his own articles, casually and with confidence, as though each queer item were an outlying promontory of the vast continent of his universal knowledge. Moreover the necessity under which he labours of always being readable tempts him at all costs to be original and unusual. Is it to be wondered at if, knowing five lines each of Virgil and Apollinaris, he prefers to quote the latter? Or if, knowing none of Virgil, he turns his ignorance into a critical virtue and lets it be understood that the best minds have now gone on from Maro to Sidonius?

In the monastery of Subiaco, which lies in that remote back of beyond behind Tivoli, there are, among many other things of beauty and historical interest, a number of frescoes by a thirteenth-century master, unknown except as the author of these works, called Conxolus. The name is superb and could not be improved. Majestic and at the same time slightly grotesque, uncommon (indeed, for all I know, unique) and easily memorable, it is a name which seems by right to belong to a great man. Conxolus: at the sound of those rich syllables the cultured person has a vague uncomfortable feeling that he ought to know what they connote. Is it a battle? or scholastic philosophy? or a heresy? or what? Learning, after a moment's agonizing suspense (during which he is uncertain whether his interlocutor will let out the secret or force him to confess his ignorance), that Conxolus was a painter, the cultured person confidently plunges. "Such a *mar*vellous artist!" he rapturously exclaims.

The old journalistic Adam is not quite dead within me, and I know my cultured society. The temptation was strong. I would preach Conxolus to a benighted world and, exalting him as an artist, exalt myself at the same time as an art critic. And how cheaply! For the price of three gallons of petrol, ten francs of post cards and tips, and an excellent lunch, with trout, at Tivoli, I should have made myself completely master of my subject and established my *Kunstforscher's* reputation. No tiresome journeys to faraway galleries in search of the master's minor works, no laborious reading of German monographs. Just this one extremely agreeable trip to the upper Anio, this forty minutes' walk uphill, this little trot round Saint Benedict's first hermitage—and that was all. I would go back to London, I would write some articles, or even a little book, with handsome reproductions, about the master. And when, in cultured society, people talked of Duccio or Simone Martini, I should smile from the height of my superiority. "They are all very well, no doubt. But when one has seen Conxolus." And I should go on talking of his tactile and olfactory values, his magistral treatment of the fourth dimension, his exquisitely subtle use of *repoussoirs* and that extraordinary mastery of colour which enabled him to paint all the flesh in his pictures in two tones of ochre, impure purple and goose-turd green. And my auditors (terrified, as all the frequenters of cultured society always are, of being left behind in the intellectual race) would listen with grave avidity. And they would leave me, triumphantly conscious that they had scored a point over their rivals, that they had entered a new swim from which all but the extremely select were excluded, that their minds were dressed in a fashion that came straight from Paris (for of course I should give them to understand that Derain and Matisse entirely agreed with me); and from that day forth the name of Conxolus, and with it my name, would begin to reverberate, *crescendo*, with an ever-growing rumour of admiration, in all the best drawing-rooms, from Euston to the World's End.

The temptation was strong; but I wrestled with it heroically and at last had the mastery. I decided that I would not pervert the truth for the sake of any reputation, however flattering, for critical insight and discrimination. For the truth, alas, is that our unique and high-sounding Conxolus is an entirely negligible painter. Competent and well-trained; but no more. His principal merit consists in the fact that he lived in the thirteenth century and worked in the characteristic style of his period. He painted in the decadent Byzantine manner which we, arguing backwards from sixteenth-century Florence instead of forwards from sixth-century Ravenna, miscall "primitive." It is in this, I repeat, that his principal merit consists— at any rate for us. For a century ago his primitiveness would only have aroused derision and pity. We have changed all that nowadays; and so thoroughly that there are many young people who, in their anxiety not to be thought old-fashioned, regard all pictures bearing a close resemblance to their subjects as highly suspicious and, unless guaranteed chemically pure by some recognized aesthetic authority, *a priori* ridiculous. To these ascetics all natural beauty, when reproduced by art, is damnable. A beautiful woman accurately painted is "chocolate boxy"; a beautiful landscape mere poetry. If a work of art is obviously charming, if it moves at first sight, then, according to these people, it must also necessarily be bad. This doctrine applied to music has led to the exaltation of Bach, even Bach in his most mechanical and soulless moments, at the expense of Beethoven. It has led to the dry "classical" way of playing Mozart, who is supposed to be unemotional because he is not vulgarly emotional, like Wagner. It has led to steam organ-like performances of Handel and senseless bellowings of Palestrina.

And the absurd young, in reaction against the sentimentalities and lachrymose idealisms which they imagine to have characterized the later Victorian age, being left absolutely unmoved by these performances, have for that very reason applauded them as in the highest degree artistic. It is the same in painting. The muddier the colours, the more distorted the figures, the higher the art. There are hundreds of young painters who dare not paint realistically and charmingly, even if they could, for fear of losing the esteem of the young connoisseurs who are their patrons. True, good painters paint well and express all they have to say whatever convention they may use; and indifferent painters paint indifferently in all circumstances. It ought, therefore, to give us no concern whatever if indifferent young painters do prefer distortion and muddy colouring to gaiety, realism and charm. It does not seriously matter how they paint. At the same time the world did get a certain amount of entertainment out of its indifferent painters in the past, when they did their best to imitate nature and tell stories. It got faithful copies of beautiful objects, it got documents and pictorial notes, it got amusing anecdotes and comments on life. These things might not be great pictures; but they

were at any rate worth something, for they
had an other than aesthetic value. Aiming
as he does at some mythical ideal of pure
aestheticism, to which all but form is sacrificed, the young talentless painter of the
present time gives us nothing but boredom.
For his pictures are not good pictures, and
they do not make amends for their badness
by reminding us of pleasing objects; they
have not even the merit of being documents
or comments, they do not even tell a story.
In a word, they have nothing to recommend
them. From being an entertainer, the second-rate artist (if he happens also to be "ad-
vanced") has become an intolerable bore.

The young's mistrust of realism does not
apply only to contemporary art; it is also
retrospective. Of two equally untalented
artists of the past youth unhesitatingly prefers the man who is least realistic, most
"primitive." Conxolus is admired above his
seventeenth-century counterpart, simply because his figures remind one of nothing that
is charming in nature, because he is innocent
of light and shade, because the composition
is rigidly symmetrical, and because the emotional content of his ardently Christian pictures has, for us, completely evaporated,
leaving nothing that can evoke in our bosoms
the slightest sentiment of any kind, with the

single exception of those famous aesthetic emotions which the young so studiously cultivate.

True, the convention in which the seventeenth-century Italian painters worked was an intolerable one. The wild gesticulations with which they filled their pictures, in the hope of artificially creating an atmosphere of passion, is fundamentally ludicrous. The baroque style and the kindred romantic style are the two styles best fitted in the nature of things for the expression of comedy. Aristophanes, Rabelais, Nashe, Balzac, Dickens, Rowlandson, Goya, Doré, Daumier, and the nameless makers of grotesques all over the world and at every period—all practitioners of pure comedy, whether in literature or in art—have employed an extravagant, baroque, romantic style. Naturally; for pure comedy it is essentially extravagant and enormous. Except in the hands of prodigious men of genius (such as Marlowe and Shakespeare, Michelangelo and Rembrandt) this style, when used for serious purposes, is ludicrous. Almost all baroque art and almost all the kindred romantic art of a later epoch are grotesque because the artists (not of the first order) are trying to express something tragic in terms of a style essentially comic. In this respect the works of the "primitives"—even of the second-rate primitives—are really preferable to the works of their *seicento* descendants. For in their pictures there is no fundamental incongruity between the style and subject. But this is a negative quality; second-rate primitives are decent but they are extraordinarily dull. The work of the later realists may be vulgar and absurd as a whole; but it is redeemed, very often, by the charm of its details. You can find, in the pictures of second-rate artists of the seventeenth century, charming landscapes, interesting physiognomies, studies of curious effects of light and shade—things which do nothing, it is true, to redeem these works, viewed as wholes, from badness, but are nevertheless agreeable and interesting in themselves. In the Conxoluses of an earlier epoch the work as a whole is respectable; but its dullness is not relieved by any curious or delightful details. By their absurdly ascetic distrust of the obviously delightful, the young have deprived themselves of a great deal of pleasure. They bore themselves by second-rate Conxoluses when they might amuse themselves by equally second-rate Fetis and Caravaggios and Rosa da Tivolis and Carpionis and Guercinos and Luca Giordanos and all the rest of them. If one must look at second-rate pictures at all

238 ESSAYS NEW AND OLD

—and there are so few good pictures that one inevitably must—it is surely more reasonable to look at those which give one something (even though the plums be embedded in a suet of horror) than those which give one absolutely nothing at all.

THE IMPORTANCE OF BEING NORDIC

NOT much balderdash is talked about organic chemistry. For the simple reason that few people who do not know something of the subject are tempted, or have the impertinence, to talk about it.

But about the infinitely more obscure and complicated subjects of human nature, heredity, racial characteristics, progress and degeneracy, the majority of us feel no diffidence. Without possessing the slightest real, systematic knowledge of these matters, we are prepared to talk of them—to talk at length, confidently and with fanatical passion.

Nobody imagines that, because his body is a walking chemical laboratory, he is therefore qualified to talk about chemistry; or that, being built up of atoms, he is for that reason an expert physicist. But we are all ready, on the mere strength of our humanity—just because we are human beings—to hold forth dogmatically on the subject of Man, of Sex, Race, Progress and all the other glorious words which that curious race

of beings known as publicists love to spell
with the largest capital letters. On the mere
strength of our humanity, I repeat; not because we know anything. Just because we
are men, we think ourselves qualified to talk
about Man. Is it to be wondered at if our
talk is, for the most part, pure and unadul-
terated bosh?

On no anthropological subject have greater
quantities of balderdash been uttered than on
the subject of racial characteristics and racial
degeneracy. The muddy stream of bosh flows
intermittently, now fast, now slow, according to the pseudo-scientific fads and the political prejudices of the moment. At the
present time it is in full spate, particularly
on the American side of the Atlantic, where
the political problems of immigration have
stimulated the anthropological philosophers
to tremendous efforts. In present-day America a handsome living is to be made by writing books about the racial characteristics of
Europeans—solemn dogmatic books, full of
perfectly groundless generalizations, which
are immensely popular with "thoughtful
readers," because they happen to fit in with
the political prejudices of the moment. From
the books, some of this intellectual swill
sloshes over into the newspapers. The jour-
nalists spice it with their sensationalism and

the public greedily laps it up. So the great work of enlightenment goes on.

Successful nations, like successful individuals, find it very difficult to believe that they are ever wrong; success, to them, is the sufficient proof of their intellectual and moral superiority. They therefore exalt the qualities which made for their own success, setting them up as a standard of absolute excellence. Races with different qualities, particularly if they happen not to be very successful at the moment, are regarded as lower races. Thus, the clever Greeks and the efficient, military Romans regarded all their neighbours as barbarians. But the word "barbarian" did not possess, for the two peoples, quite the same connotation. To the Greeks it signified primarily a stupid, unscientific, unphilosophical man (a Roman, for example). To the Romans it implied lack of discipline, inefficiency, bad organization. In the course of history there have been many standards of racial virtue, set up by many races.

The Nordic races have now, in their own imagination, taken the place of the Greeks and Romans. All virtue and intelligence belong to them; all that is bad to the Mediterranean and Alpine races. Historians may venture to suggest that the Athenians were no fools, that Julius Caesar and Napoleon were remarkable men, that the Italians of the Renaissance achieved a thing or two. "That was because they were all Nordic," the anthropological philosophers reply. "How do you make that out?" we ask in some surprise. "They must have been Nordic," the philosophers answer, "because they did such remarkable things." We sink beneath the weight of argument.

It is a very long time since I read Mr. Houston Chamberlain's immortal work on these great subjects. But so far as I remember he contrived to prove decisively that not only Napoleon, but also Jesus Christ was of Teutonic origin. The Great War has been fought since Mr. Houston Chamberlain wrote his book. Naturally we can't expect anthropological philosophy to be the same to-day as it was in Houston's time. And it isn't. Since the war, certain American philosophers have made the epoch-making discovery that the Germans are not Nordic at all. Why not? Because, if they had been, they could not have behaved as they did. Q. E. D.

What nonsense it all is! Even the more cautious generalizations of those who do not go so far as to affirm the Nordicity of Napoleon and Jesus of Nazareth, are still without foundation. These less extreme theorists are prepared to admit that the Mediterranean peoples were bright enough in their day; but they insist that they are now degenerate and should not, therefore, be allowed to contaminate by their presence the lands in which the all-virtuous, all-intelligent Nordics live. The compatriots of Dante, Michelangelo and Galileo are permitted by the new immigration laws of the United States to send only a few hundred of their annual increase of population into the great Nordic land. They are an inferior race; they are degenerates.

Degenerate. . . . It is a fine reverberating word. And a most convenient word to throw at people you don't like. For example, you don't like post-impressionism; therefore Matisse is degenerate. You think St. Francis was a fool because he didn't go on the Stock Exchange and make a large fortune; he was a degenerate. German beer gives you indigestion; you object to the rapacity of French hotel-keepers—these races (who can doubt it?) are degenerate. And so on. There are few more useful words in the whole dictionary.

Now if the word "degeneracy" means anything (beyond the fact, of course, that you dislike the race or the individual to whom you apply it) it connotes an inherited and heritable quality. In zoology, degeneration means the progressive simplification of forms. Thus, many parasites are degenerates from non-parasitic ancestors having much more complicated and highly developed structures. When you say, therefore, that the Italians, for example, have degenerated from what they were in the days of Michelangelo, you mean—if you mean anything, which is in no way essential in these deep discussions—that they are now born different from what they were four hundred years ago, and that they are passing on this difference to their off-spring. Now, if this is the case, the evolution of man must be utterly unlike that of all other animals. For in no other animal is the slightest specific change apparent after a lapse of only ten or twelve generations. If men degenerate so quickly, we might expect dogs and cats to do the same. But so far as I am aware, no cynological philosopher has arisen to denounce the abject degeneracy of the Irish terrier, the French bulldog, the sheepdog of the Maremma, the manifestly non-Nordic dachshund, and that sinister mixture of Teutonic and Mediterranean, the Alsatian wolf-hound.

The fact of the matter is that all the phenomena of so-called degeneracy are either imaginary—being invented by foreign observers who do not happen to like the characteristics of the race to which they attribute degeneracy—or, if real, are due to external causes which, though they may influence the life and habits of several generations of men and women, are quite powerless (acquired characteristics not being heritable) to affect the specific character of the race.

Let us take the obvious case of the Italians. The amateur anthropologists call them degenerate. Why? On the ground, chiefly, that they have failed to produce as many great artists during the nineteenth century as they did in the fifteenth and sixteenth. True; but the anthropologists forget to remark that during the first two-thirds of the nineteenth century the Italians were busily engaged in freeing their country from foreign oppressors and that since 1870 they have been at work on the exploitation of an, industrially speaking, brand-new country, the gradual creation of a great European state and the political education of a people habituated to foreign tyranny. These are labours requiring considerable ability to perform.

Ability is of two kinds—general and special. Special ability may be combined with general ability, or it may not. A man may be an extraordinary mathematician, painter, musician, chess player, and in all other respects almost an imbecile. Claude Lorraine, for example, could not learn to read or write. The man with a highly developed special ability ought not and often cannot do anything but what he is peculiarly fitted by nature to do. But the man of general ability can do almost anything he chooses to set his mind to. His choice of a career is largely a matter of accident. Now, at the time of the Renaissance, it happened that the political, social and religious conditions in Italy were such that the greatest part of the existing general ability was turned into artistic channels. In the first two-thirds of the nineteenth century, almost all the general ability of the Italian people was absorbed in the struggle for liberty. Since 1870 it has been absorbed in the development of a politically and industrially new country. Nobody blames the Americans or the Australians for not having produced, within the first century of their existence, an Elizabethan or a Medicean age. It is recognized that they have had no time to do anything but develop the material prosperity of their countries. But to the Italians no such indulgence is allowed. And yet they have had a far more difficult problem to solve than the Americans or the Australians. They have had to create an efficient government among the victims of century-long foreign oppression. They have had to develop, not a huge, rich and unpopulated land, but a small, poor and crowded one. All things being considered, it seems to me that they have done a difficult job remarkably well. And they have found time, in the midst of their labour, to produce a respectable quantity of literature, music and pure science. A little of that energy and ability which, in another epoch and in different circumstances, produced the artistic and speculative triumphs of the Renaissance, still flows along the old channels. But the greater part of the ability has been diverted. The artists have turned into engineers, politicians and business men. The ability which made the Renaissance is now making modern Italy.

I have spoken dogmatically, as though I knew the whole truth about the Italian character, human ability and all the rest. But of course, as a matter of fact, I know just as little of these matters as the philosophers who dogmatize about the degeneracy of the Mediterranean race and the supremacy of the Nordic—that is to say, precisely nothing. All that I claim for my dogmatisms is that they do not so obviously contradict the facts of history and the ascertained truths and probabilities of science as do theirs. The best would be, of course, not to dogmatize at all, until we know something about these fascinating and portentously difficult subjects.

The proper study of mankind, the poet tells us, is man. The proper *study*. He did not say that it was the proper subject to hold dogmatic and utterly unfounded opinions about. By all means let us study Man—study him patiently, scientifically, with humility and suspense of judgment, until we have some data on which to base reasonable opinions. Meanwhile the ignorant dogmatists —such as myself and, on the other side, the numerous successors of Mr. Houston Chamberlain—would do well to hold their tongues. The noise we make tends to distract the serious students.

CHAUCER

THERE are few things more melancholy than the spectacle of literary fossilization. A great writer comes into being, lives, labours and dies. Time passes; year by year the sediment of muddy comment and criticism thickens round the great man's bones. The sediment sets firm; what was once a living organism becomes a thing of marble. On the attainment of total fossilization the great man has become a classic. It becomes increasingly difficult for the members of each succeeding generation to remember that the stony objects which fill the museum cases were once alive. It is often a work of considerable labour to reconstruct the living animal from the fossil shape. But the trouble is generally worth taking. And in no case is it more worth while than in Chaucer's.

With Chaucer the ordinary fossilizing process, to which every classical author is subject, has been complicated by the petrifaction of his language. Five hundred years have almost sufficed to turn the most living of poets into a substitute on the modern sides of schools for the metal gymnastic of Latin and Greek. Prophetically, Chaucer saw the fate that awaited him and appealed against his doom:

> Ye know eke that, in form of speech is change
> Within a thousand years, and wordes tho
> That hadden price, now wonder nice and strange
> Us thinketh them; and yet they spake them so,
> And sped as well in love as men now do.

The body of his poetry may have grown old, but its spirit is still young and immortal. To know that spirit—and not to know it is to ignore something that is of unique importance in the history of our literature—it is necessary to make the effort of becoming familiar with the body it informs and gives life to. The antique language and versification, so "wonder nice and strange" to our ears, are obstacles in the path of most of those who read for pleasure's sake (not that any reader worthy of the name ever reads for anything else but pleasure); to the pedants they are an end in themselves. Theirs is the carcass, but not the soul. Between those who are daunted by his superficial difficulties and those who take too much delight in them Chaucer finds but few sympathetic readers. I hope in these pages to be able to give a few of the reasons that make Chaucer so well worth reading.

Chaucer's art is, by its very largeness and objectiveness, extremely difficult to subject to critical analysis. Confronted by it, Dryden could only exclaim, "Here is God's plenty!"—and the exclamation proves, when all is said, to be the most adequate and satisfying of all criticisms. All that the critic can hope to do is to expand and to illustrate Dryden's exemplary brevity.

"God's plenty!"—the phrase is a peculiarly happy one. It calls up a vision of the prodigal earth, of harvest fields, of innumerable beasts and birds, of teeming life. And it is in the heart of this living and material world of Nature that Chaucer lives. He is the poet of earth, supremely content to walk, desiring no wings. Many English poets have loved the earth for the sake of something—a dream, a reality, call it which you will—that lies behind it. But there have been few, and, except for Chaucer, no poets of greatness, who have been in love with earth for its own sake, with Nature in the sense of something inevitably material, something that is the opposite of the supernatural. Supreme over everything in this world he sees the natural order, the "law of kind," as he calls it. The teachings of most of the great prophets and poets are simply protests against the law of kind. Chaucer does not protest, he accepts. It is precisely this acceptance that makes him unique among English poets. He does not go to Nature as the symbol of some further spiritual reality; hills, flowers, sea, and clouds are not, for him, transparencies through which the workings of a great soul are visible. No, they are opaque; he likes them for what they are, things pleasant and beautiful, and not the less delicious because they are definitely of the earth earthy. Human beings, in the same way, he takes as he finds, noble and beastish, but, on the whole, wonderfully decent. He has none of that strong ethical bias which is usually to be found in the English mind. He is not horrified by the behaviour of his fellow-beings, and he has no desire to reform them. Their characters, their motives interest him, and he stands looking on at them, a happy spectator. This serenity of detachment, this placid acceptance of things and people as they are, is emphasized if we compare the poetry of Chaucer with that of his contemporary Langland, or whoever it was that wrote *Piers Plowman.*

The historians tell us that the later years of the fourteenth century were among the most disagreeable periods of our national history. English prosperity was at a very low ebb. The Black Death had exterminated nearly a third of the working population of the islands, a fact which, aggravated by the frenzied legislation of the Government, had led to the unprecedented labour troubles that culminated in the peasant's revolt. Clerical corruption and lawlessness were rife. All things considered, even our own age is preferable to that in which Chaucer lived. Langland does not spare denunciation; he is appalled by the wickedness about him, scandalized at the openly confessed vices that have almost ceased to pay to virtue the tribute of hypocrisy. Indignation is the inspiration of *Piers Plowman*, the righteous indignation of the prophet. But to read Chaucer one would imagine that there was nothing in fourteenth-century England to be indignant about. It is true that the Pardoner, the Friar, the Shipman, the Miller, and, in fact, most of the Canterbury pilgrims are rogues and scoundrels; but, then, they are such "merry harlots" too. It is true that the Monk prefers hunting to praying, that, in these latter days when fairies are no more, "there is none other incubus" but the friar, that "purse is the Archdeacon's hell," and the Summoner a villain of the first magnitude; but Chaucer can only regard these things as primarily humorous. The fact of people not practising what they preach is an unfailing source of amusement to him.

Where Langland cries aloud in anger, threatening the world with hell-fire, Chaucer looks on and smiles. To the great political crisis of his time he makes but one reference, and that a comic one:

> So hideous was the noyse, ah *benedicite!*
> Certes he Jakke Straw, and his meyné,
> Ne maden schoutes never half so schrille,
> Whan that they wolden eny Flemyng kille,
> As thilke day was mad upon the fox.

Peasants may revolt, priests break their vows, lawyers lie and cheat, and the world in general indulge its sensual appetites; why try and prevent them, why protest? After all, they are all simply being natural, they are all following the law of kind. A reasonable man, like himself, "flees fro the pres and dwelles with soothfastnesse." But reasonable men are few, and it is the nature of human beings to be the unreasonable sport of instinct and passion, just as it is the nature of the daisy to open its eye to the sun, and of the goldfinch to be a spritely and "gaylard" creature. The law of kind has always and in everything domination; there is no rubbing nature against the hair. For

> God it wot, there may no man embrace
> As to destreyne a thing, the which nature
> Hath naturelly set in a creature.

Take any brid, and put him in a cage,
And do all thine entent and thy corrage
To foster it tendrely with meat and drynke,
And with alle the deyntees thou canst bethinke,
And keep it all so kyndly as thou may;
Although his cage of gold be never so gay,
Yet hath this brid, by twenty thousand fold,
Lever in a forest, that is wyld and cold,
Gon ete wormes, and such wrecchidnes;
For ever this brid will doon his busynes
To scape out of his cage when that he may;
His liberté the brid desireth aye . . .
Lo, heer hath kynd his dominacioun,
And appetyt flemeth (banishes) discrescioun.
Also a she wolf hath a vilayne kynde,
The lewideste wolf that she may fynde,
Or least of reputacioun, him will sche take,
In tyme whan hir lust to have a make.
Alle this ensaumples tell I by these men
That ben untrewe, and nothing by wommen.

(As the story from which these lines are
quoted happens to be about an unfaithful
wife, it seems that, in making the female sex
immune from the action of the law of kind,
Chaucer is indulging a little in irony.)

For men han ever a licorous appetit
On lower thing to parforme her delit
Than on her wyves, ben they never so faire,
Ne never so trewe, ne so debonaire.

Nature, deplorable as some of its manifestations may be, must always and inevitably
assert itself. The law of kind has power

even over immortal souls. This fact is the source of the poet's constantly expressed dislike of celibacy and asceticism. The doctrine that upholds the superiority of the state of virginity over that of wedlock is, to begin with (he holds), a danger to the race. It encourages a process which we may be permitted to call dysgenics—the carrying on of the species by the worst members. The Host's words to the Monk are memorable:

Allas! why wearest thou so wide a cope?
God give me sorwe! and I were a pope
Nought only thou, but every mighty man,
Though he were shore brode upon his pan (head)
Should han a wife; for all this world is lorn;
Religioun hath take up all the corn
Of tredyng, and we burel (humble) men ben
    shrimpes;
Of feble trees there cometh wrecchid impes.
This maketh that our heires ben so sclendere
And feble, that they may not wel engendre.

But it is not merely dangerous; it is antinatural. That is the theme of the Wife of Bath's Prologue. Counsels of perfection are all very well when they are given to those

That wolde lyve parfytly;
But, lordyngs, by your leve, that am not I.

The bulk of us must live as the law of kind enjoins.

It is characteristic of Chaucer's conception of the world, that the highest praise he can bestow on anything is to assert of it, that it possesses in the highest degree the qualities of its own particular kind.   Thus of Cressida he says:

> She was not with the least of her stature,
> But all her limbes so well answering
> Weren to womanhood, that creature
> Nas never lesse mannish in seeming.

The horse of brass in the *Squire's Tale* is

> So well proportioned to be strong,
> Right as it were a steed of Lombardye,
> Thereto so *horsely* and so quick of eye.

Everything that is perfect of its kind is admirable, even though the kind may not be an exalted one.   It is, for instance, a joy to see the way in which the Canon sweats:

> A cloote-leaf (dock leaf) he had under his hood
> For sweat, and for to keep his head from heat.
> But it was joye for to see him sweat;
> His forehead dropped as a stillatorie
> Were full of plantain or of peritorie.

The Canon is supreme in the category of sweaters, the very type and idea of perspiring humanity; therefore he is admirable and joyous to behold, even as a horse that is supremely horsely or a woman less mannish than anything one could imagine.   In the same way it is a delight to behold the Pardoner preaching to the people.   In its own kind his charlatanism is perfect and deserves admiration:

> Mine handes and my tonge gon so yerne,
> That it is joye to see my busynesse.

This manner of saying of things that they are joyous, or, very often, heavenly, is typical of Chaucer.   He looks out on the world with a delight that never grows old or weary.   The sights and sounds of daily life, all the lavish beauty of the earth fill him with a pleasure which he can only express by calling it a "joy" or a "heaven."   It "joye was to see" Cressida and her maidens playing together; and

> So aungellyke was her native beauté
> That like a thing immortal seemede she,
> As doth an heavenish parfit creature.

The peacock has angel's feathers; a girl's voice is heavenly to hear:

> Antigone the shene
> Gan on a Trojan song to singen clear,
> That it an heaven was her voice to hear.

One could go on indefinitely multiplying quotations that testify to Chaucer's exquisite sensibility to sensuous beauty and his immediate, almost exclamatory response to it. Above all, he is moved by the beauty of "young, fresh folkes, he and she"; by the grace and swiftness of living things, birds and animals; by flowers and placid, luminous, park-like landscapes.

It is interesting to note how frequently Chaucer speaks of animals. Like many other sages, he perceives that an animal is, in a certain sense, more human in character than a man. For an animal bears the same relation to a man as a caricature to a portrait. In a way a caricature is truer than a portrait. It reveals all the weaknesses and absurdities that flesh is heir to. The portrait brings out the greatness and dignity of the spirit that inhabits the often ridiculous flesh. It is not merely that Chaucer has written regular fables, though the *Nun's Priest's Tale* puts him among the great fabulists of the world, and there is also much definitely fabular matter in the *Parliament of Fowls*. No, his references to the beasts are not confined to his animal stories alone; they are scattered broadcast throughout his works. He relies for much of his psychology and for much of his most vivid description on the comparison of man, in his character and appearance (which with Chaucer are al-

ways indissolubly blended), with the beasts.
Take, for example, that enchanting simile in
which Troilus, stubbornly anti-natural in re-
fusing to love as the law of kind enjoins
him, is compared to the corn-fed horse, who
has to be taught good behaviour and sound
philosophy under the whip:

> As proude Bayard ginneth for to skip
> Out of the way, so pricketh him his corn,
> Till he a lash have of the longe whip,
> Then thinketh he, "Though I prance all biforn,
> First in the trace, full fat and newe shorn,
> Yet am I but an horse, and horses' law
> I must endure and with my feeres draw."

Or, again, women with too pronounced a
taste for fine apparel are likened to the cat:

> And if the cattes skin be sleek and gay,
> She will not dwell in housé half a day,
> But forth she will, ere any day be dawet
> To show her skin and gon a caterwrawet.

In his descriptions of the personal appearance of his characters Chaucer makes constant use of animal characteristics. Human
beings, both beautiful and hideous, are
largely described in terms of animals. It is
interesting to see how often in that exquisite
description of Alisoun, the carpenter's wife,
Chaucer produces his clearest and sharpest
effects by a reference to some beast or bird:

Fair was this younge wife, and therewithal
As any weasel her body gent and small . . .
But of her song it was as loud and yern
As is the swallow chittering on a barn.
Thereto she coulde skip and make a game
As any kid or calf following his dame.
Her mouth was sweet as bragot is or meath,
Or hoard of apples, laid in hay or heath.
Wincing she was, as is a jolly colt,
Long as a mast and upright as a bolt.

Again and again in Chaucer's poems do we find such similitudes, and the result is always a picture of extraordinary precision and liveliness. Here, for example, are a few:

Gaylard he was as goldfinch in the shaw,

or,

Such glaring eyen had he as an hare;

or,

As piled (bald) as an ape was his skull.

The self-indulgent friars are

Like Jovinian,
Fat as a whale, and walken as a swan.

The Pardoner describes his own preaching in these words:

Then pain I me to stretche forth my neck
And east and west upon the people I beck,
As doth a dove, sitting on a barn.

Very often, too, Chaucer derives his happiest metaphors from birds and beasts. Of Troy in its misfortune and decline he says: Fortune

> Gan pull away the feathers bright of Troy
> From day to day.

Love-sick Troilus soliloquizes thus:

> He said: "O fool, now art thou in the snare
> That whilom japedest at lovés pain,
> Now art thou hent, now gnaw thin owné chain."

The metaphor of Troy's bright feathers reminds me of a very beautiful simile borrowed from the life of the plants:

> And as in winter leavés been bereft,
> Each after other, till the tree be bare,
> So that there nis but bark and branches left,
> Lieth Troilus, bereft of each welfare,
> Ybounden in the blacke bark of care.

And this, in turn, reminds me of that couplet in which Chaucer compares a girl to a flowering pear-tree:

> She was well more blissful on to see
> Than is the newe parjonette tree.

Chaucer is as much at home among the stars as he is among the birds and beasts and flowers of earth. There are some literary men of to-day who are not merely not

ashamed to confess their total ignorance of
all facts of a "scientific" order, but even
make a boast of it. Chaucer would have regarded such persons with pity and contempt.
His own knowledge of astronomy was wide
and exact. Those whose education has been
as horribly imperfect as my own will always
find some difficulty in following him as he
moves with easy assurance through the
heavens. Still, it is possible without knowing any mathematics to appreciate Chaucer's
descriptions of the great pageant of the sun
and stars as they march in triumph from
mansion to mansion through the year. He
does not always trouble to take out his
astrolabe and measure the progress of "Phebus, with his rosy cart"; he can record the
god's movements in more general terms that
may be understood even by the literary man
of nineteen hundred and twenty. Here, for
example, is a description of "the colde frosty
seisoun of Decembre," in which matters ce-
lestial and earthly are mingled to make a
picture of extraordinary richness:

Phebus wox old and hewed like latoun,
That in his hoté declinacioun
Shone as the burned gold, with streames bright;
But now in Capricorn adown he light,
Where as he shone full pale; I dare well sayn
The bitter frostes with the sleet and rain

Destroyed hath the green in every yerd.
Janus sit by the fire with double beard,
And drinketh of his bugle horn the wine;
Beforn him stont the brawn of tusked swine,
And *"noel"* cryeth every lusty man.

In astrology he does not seem to have believed. The magnificent passage in the *Man
of Law's Tale*, where it is said that

In the starres, clearer than is glass,
Is written, God wot, whoso can it read,
The death of every man withouten drede,

is balanced by the categorical statement
found in the scientific and educational treatise on the astrolabe, that judicial astrology
is mere deceit.

His scepticism with regard to astrology is
not surprising. Highly as he prizes authority, he prefers the evidence of experience,
and where that evidence is lacking he is content to profess a quiet agnosticism. His respect for the law of kind is accompanied by
a complementary mistrust of all that does
not appear to belong to the natural order of
things. There are moments when he doubts
even the fundamental beliefs of the Church:

A thousand sythes have I herd men telle
That there is joye in heaven and peyne in helle;
And I accorde well that it be so.
But natheless, this wot I well also
That there is none that dwelleth in this countree
That either hath in helle or heaven y-be.

Of the fate of the spirit after death he speaks
in much the same style:

His spiryt changed was, and wente there
As I came never, I cannot tellen where;
Therefore I stint, I nam no divinistre;
Of soules fynde I not in this registre,
Ne me list not th' opiniouns to telle
Of hem, though that they witten where they dwelle.

He has no patience with superstitions. Belief in dreams, in auguries, fear of the
"ravenes qualm or schrychynge of thise
owles" are all unbefitting to a self-respecting
man:

To trowen on it bothe false and foul is;
Alas, alas, so noble a creature
As is a man shall dreaden such ordure!

By an absurd pun he turns all Calchas's
magic arts of prophecy to ridicule:

So when this Calkas knew by calkulynge,
And eke by answer of this Apollo
That Grekes sholden such a people bringe,
Through which that Troye muste ben fordo,
He cast anon out of the town to go.

It would not be making a fanciful comparison to say that Chaucer in many respects
resembles Anatole France. Both men possess
a profound love of this world for its own
sake, coupled with a profound and gentle
scepticism about all that lies beyond this

world. To both of them the lavish beauty of Nature is a never-failing and all-sufficient source of happiness. Neither of them is an ascetic; in pain and privation they see nothing but evil. To both of them the notion that self-denial and self-mortification are necessarily righteous and productive of good is wholly alien. Both of them are apostles of sweetness and light, of humanity and reasonableness. Unbounded tolerance of human weakness and a pity, not the less sincere for being a little ironical, characterize them both. Deep knowledge of the evils and horrors of this unintelligible world makes them all the more attached to its kindly beauty. But in at least one important respect Chaucer shows himself to be the greater, the completer spirit. He possesses, what Anatole France does not, an imaginative as well as an intellectual comprehension of things. Faced by the multitudinous variety of human character, Anatole France exhibits a curious impotence of imagination. He does not understand characters in the sense that, say, Tolstoy understands them; he cannot, by the power of imagination, get inside them, become what he contemplates. None of the persons of his creation are complete characters; they cannot be looked at from every side; they are portrayed, as it were, in the flat and not in three dimensions. But Chaucer has the power of getting into some one else's character. His understanding of the men and women of whom he writes is complete; his slightest character sketches are always solid and three-dimensional. The Prologue to the *Canterbury Tales*, in which the effects are almost entirely produced by the description of external physical features, furnishes us with the most obvious example of his three-dimensional drawing. Or, again, take that description in the *Merchant's Tale* of old January and his young wife May after their wedding night. It is wholly a description of external details, yet the result is not a superficial picture. We are given a glimpse of the characters in their entirety:

Thus laboureth he till that the day gan dawe,
And then he taketh a sop in fine clarré,
And upright in his bed then sitteth he.
And after that he sang full loud and clear,
And kissed his wife and made wanton cheer.
He was all coltish, full of ragerye,
And full of jargon as a flecked pye.
The slacké skin about his necké shaketh,
While that he sang, so chanteth he and craketh.
But God wot what that May thought in her heart,
When she him saw up sitting in his shirt,
In his night cap and with his necke lean;
She praiseth not his playing worth a bean.

But these are all slight sketches. For full-length portraits of character we must turn to *Troilus and Cressida*, a work which, though it was written before the fullest maturity of Chaucer's powers, is in many ways his most remarkable achievement, and one, moreover, which has never been rivalled for beauty and insight in the whole field of English narrative poetry. When one sees with what certainty and precision Chaucer describes every movement of Cressida's spirit from the first moment she hears of Troilus' love for her to the moment when she is unfaithful to him, one can only wonder why the novel of character should have been so slow to make its appearance. It was not until the eighteenth century that narrative artists, using prose as their medium instead of verse, began to rediscover the secrets that were familiar to Chaucer in the fourteenth.

Troilus and Cressida was written, as we have said, before Chaucer had learnt to make the fullest use of his powers. In colouring it is fainter, less sharp and brilliant than the best of the *Canterbury Tales*. The character studies are there, carefully and accurately worked out; but we miss the bright vividness of presentation with which Chaucer was to endow his later art. The characters are all alive and completely seen and understood.

But they move, as it were, behind a veil—the veil of that poetic convention which had, in the earliest poems, almost completely shrouded Chaucer's genius, and which, as he grew up, as he adventured and discovered, grew thinner and thinner, and finally vanished like gauzy mist in the sunlight. When *Troilus and Cressida* was written the mist had not completely dissipated, and the figures of his creation, complete in conception and execution as they are, are seen a little dimly because of the interposed veil.

The only moment in the poem when Chaucer's insight seems to fail him is at the very end; he has to account for Cressida's unfaithfulness, and he is at a loss to know how he shall do it. Shakespeare, when he rehandled the theme, had no such difficulty. His version of the story, planned on much coarser lines than Chaucer's, leads obviously and inevitably to the fore-ordained conclusion; his Cressida is a minx who simply lives up to her character. What could be more simple? But to Chaucer the problem is not so simple. His Cressida is not a minx. From the moment he first sets eyes on her, Chaucer, like his own unhappy Troilus, falls head over ears in love. Beautiful, gentle, gay; possessing, it is true, somewhat "tendre wittes," but making up for her lack of skill in ratiocination by the "sudden avysements" of intuition; vain, but not disagreeably so, of her good looks and of her power over so great and noble a knight as Troilus; slow to feel love, but once she has yielded, rendering back to Troilus passion for passion; in a word, the "least mannish" of all possible creatures—she is to Chaucer the ideal of gracious and courtly womanhood. But, alas, the old story tells us that Cressida jilted her Troilus for that gross prize-fighter of a man, Diomed. The woman whom Chaucer has made his ideal proves to be no better than she should be; there is a flaw in the crystal. Chaucer is infinitely reluctant to admit the fact. But the old story is specific in its statement; indeed, its whole point consists in Cressida's infidelity. Called upon to explain his heroine's fall, Chaucer is completely at a loss. He makes a few half-hearted attempts to solve the problem, and then gives it up, falling back on authority. The old clerks say it was so, therefore it must be so, and that's that. The fact is that Chaucer pitched his version of the story in a different key from that which is found in the "olde bokes," with the result that the note on which he is compelled by his respect for authority to close is completely out of harmony with the rest of the music. It is this that accounts for the chief, and indeed the only defect of the poem—its hurried and boggled conclusion.

I cannot leave Cressida without some mention of the doom which was prepared for her by one of Chaucer's worthiest disciples, Robert Henryson, in some ways the best of the Scottish poets of the fifteenth and sixteenth centuries. Shocked by the fact that, in Chaucer's poem, Cressida receives no punishment for her infidelity, Henryson composed a short sequel, *The Testament of Cresseid*, to show that poetic justice was duly performed. Diomed, we are told, grew weary as soon as he had "all his appetyte and mair, fulfillit on this fair ladie," and cast her off, to become a common drab.

> O fair Cresseid! the flour and *A per se*
> Of Troy and Greece, how wast thow fortunait!
> To change in filth all thy feminitie
> And be with fleshly lust sa maculait,
> And go amang the Grekis, air and late
> So giglot-like.

In her misery she curses Venus and Cupid for having caused her to love only to lead her to this degradation:

> The seed of love was sowen in my face
> And ay grew green through your supply and grace.
> But now, alas! that seed with frost is slain,
> And I fra lovers left, and all forlane.

In revenge Cupid and his mother summon a council of gods and condemn the *A per se* of Greece and Troy to be a hideous leper. And so she goes forth with the other lepers, armed with bowl and clapper, to beg her bread. One day Troilus rides past the place where she is sitting by the roadside near the gates of Troy:

> Then upon him she cast up both her een,
>   And with ane blenk it cam into his thocht,
> That he some time before her face had seen,
>   But she was in such plight he knew her nocht,
>   Yet then her look into his mind it brocht
> The sweet visage and amorous blenking
> Of fair Cresseid, one sometime his own darling.

He throws her an alms and the poor creature dies. And so the moral sense is satisfied. There is a good deal of superfluous mythology and unnecessary verbiage in *The Testament of Cresseid*, but the main lines of the poem are firmly and powerfully drawn. Of all the disciples of Chaucer, from Hoccleve and the Monk of Bury down to Mr. Masefield, Henryson may deservedly claim to stand the highest.

POPULAR MUSIC

THERE is a certain jovial, bouncing, hoppety little tune with which any one who has spent even a few weeks in Germany, or has been tended in childhood by a German nurse, must be very familiar. Its name is "Ach, du lieber Augustin." It is a merry little affair in three-four time; in rhythm and melody so simple, that the village idiot could sing it after a first hearing; in sentiment so innocent that the heart of the most susceptible maiden would not quicken by a beat a minute at the sound of it. Rum ti-tiddle, Um tum tum, Um tum tum, Um tum tum: Rum ti-tiddle, Um tum tum, Um tum tum, TUM. By the very frankness of its cheerful imbecility the thing disarms all criticism.

Now for a piece of history. "Ach, du lieber Augustin" was composed in 1770, and it was the first waltz. The first waltz! I must ask the reader to hum the tune to himself, then to think of any modern waltz with which he may be familiar. He will find in the difference between the tunes a subject richly suggestive of interesting meditations.

The difference between "Ach, du lieber

Augustin" and any waltz tune composed at any date from the middle of the nineteenth century onwards, is the difference between one piece of music almost completely empty of emotional content and another, densely saturated with amorous sentiment, languor and voluptuousness. The susceptible maiden who, when she hears "Ach, du lieber Augustin," feels no emotions beyond a general sense of high spirits and cheerfulness, is fairly made to palpitate by the luscious strains of the modern waltz. Her soul is carried swooning along, over waves of syrup; she seems to breathe an atmosphere heavy with ambergris and musk. From the jolly little thing it was at its birth, the waltz has grown into the voluptuous, heart-stirring affair with which we are now familiar.

And what has happened to the waltz has happened to all popular music. It was once innocent but is now provocative; once pellucid, now richly clotted; once elegant, now deliberately barbarous. Compare the music of *The Beggar's Opera* with the music of a contemporary revue. They differ as life in the garden of Eden differed from life in the artistic quarter of Gomorrah. The one is prelapsarian in its airy sweetness, the other is rich, luscious and loud with conscious savagery.

The evolution of popular music has run parallel on a lower plane, with the evolution of serious music. The writers of popular tunes are not musicians enough to be able to invent new forms of expression. All they do is to adapt the discoveries of original geniuses to the vulgar taste. Ultimately and indirectly, Beethoven is responsible for all the languishing waltz tunes, all the savage jazzings, for all that is maudlin and violent in our popular music. He is responsible because it was he who first devised really effective musical methods for the direct expression of emotion. Beethoven's emotions happened to be noble; moreover, he was too intellectual a musician to neglect the formal, architectural side of music. But unhappily he made it possible for composers of inferior mind and character to express in music their less exalted passions and vulgarer emotions. He made possible the weakest sentimentalities of Schumann, the baroque grandiosities of Wagner, the hysterics of Scriabine; he made possible the waltzes of all the Strausses, from the *Blue Danube* to the waltz from *Salome*. And he made possible, at a still further remove, such masterpieces of popular art as "You Made Me Love You" and "That Coal Black Mammy of Mine."

For the introduction of a certain vibrant

sexual quality into music, Beethoven is perhaps less directly responsible than the nineteenth-century Italians. I used often to wonder why it was that Mozart's operas were less popular than those of Verdi, Leoncavallo and Puccini. You couldn't ask for more, or more infectiously "catchy" tunes than are to be found in *Figaro* or *Don Giovanni*. The music, though "classical," is not obscure, nor forbiddingly complex. On the contrary it is clear, simple with that seemingly easy simplicity which only consummate genius can achieve, and thoroughly engaging. And yet for every time *Don Giovanni* is played, *La Bohème* is played a hundred. *Tosca* is at least fifty times as popular as *Figaro*. And if you look through a catalogue of gramophone records you will find that, while you can buy *Rigoletto* complete in thirty discs, there are not more than three records of *The Magic Flute*. This seems at first sight extremely puzzling. But the reason is not really far to seek. Since Mozart's day composers have learned the art of making music throatily and palpitatingly sexual. The arias of Mozart have a beautiful clear purity which renders them utterly insipid compared with the sobbing, catch-in-the-throaty melodies of the nineteenth-century Italians. The public, having accustomed itself to this stronger and more turbid brewage, finds no flavour in the crystal songs of Mozart.

No essay on modern popular music would be complete without some grateful reference to Rossini, who was, so far as I know, the first composer to show what charms there are in vulgar melody. Melodies before Rossini's day were often exceedingly commonplace and cheap; but almost never do they possess that almost indefinable quality of low vulgarity which adorns some of the most successful of Rossini's airs, and which we recognize as being somehow a modern, contemporary quality. The methods which Rossini employed for the achievement of his melodic vulgarity are not easy to analyse. His great secret, I fancy, was the very short and easily memorable phrase frequently repeated in different parts of the scale. But it is easiest to define by example. Think of Moses' first Aria in *Moses in Egypt*. That is an essentially vulgar melody; and it is quite unlike the popular melodies of an earlier date. Its affinities are with the modern popular tune. It is to his invention of vulgar tunes that Rossini owed his enormous contemporary success. Vulgar people before his day had to be content with Mozart's delicate airs. Rossini came and revealed to them a more congenial music. That the world fell down and gratefully worshipped him is not surprising. If he has long ceased to be popular, that is because his successors, profiting by his lessons, have achieved in his own vulgar line triumphs of which he could not have dreamed.

Barbarism has entered popular music from two sources—from the music of barbarous people, like the negroes, and from serious music which has drawn upon barbarism for its inspiration. The technique of being barbarous effectively has come, of course, from serious music. In the elaboration of this technique no musicians have done more than the Russians. If Rimsky-Korsakoff had never lived, modern dance music would not be the thing it is.

Whether, having grown inured to such violent and purely physiological stimuli as the clashing and drumming, the rhythmic throbbing and wailing glissandos of modern jazz music can supply, the world will never revert to something less crudely direct, is a matter about which one cannot prophesy. Even serious musicians seem to find it hard to dispense with barbarism. In spite of the monotony and the appalling lack of subtlety which characterize the process, they persist in banging away in the old Russian manner, as though there were nothing more interesting or exciting to be thought of. When, as a boy, I first heard Russian music, I was carried off my feet by its wild melodies, its persistent, its relentlessly throbbing rhythms. But my excitement grew less and less with every hearing. To-day no music seems to me more tedious. The only music a civilized man can take unfailing pleasure in is civilized music. If you were compelled to listen every day of your life to a single piece of music, would you choose Stravinsky's "Oiseau de Feu" or Beethoven's "Grosse Fugue"? Obviously you would choose the fugue, if only for its intricacy and because there is more in it to occupy the mind than in the Russian's too simple rhythms. Composers seem to forget that we are, in spite of everything and though appearances may be against us, tolerably civilized. They overwhelm us not merely with Russian and negroid noises, but with Celtic caterwaulings on the black notes, with dismal Spanish wailings, punctuated by the rattle of the castanets and the clashing harmonies of the guitar. When serious composers have gone back to civilized music— and already some of them are turning from barbarism—we shall probably hear a corresponding change for the more refined in popular music. But until serious musicians lead the way, it will be absurd to expect the vulgarizers to change their style.

THE BEST PICTURE

BORGO SAN SEPOLCRO is not very easy to get at. There is a small low-comedy railway across the hills from Arezzo. Or you can approach it up the Tiber valley from Perugia. Or, if you happen to be at Urbino, there is a motor 'bus which takes you to San Sepolcro, up and down through the Apennines, in something over seven hours. No joke, that journey, as I know by experience. But it is worth doing, though preferably in some other vehicle than the 'bus, for the sake of the Bocca Trabaria, that most beautiful of Apennine passes, between the Tiber valley and the upper valley of the Metauro. It was in the early spring that we crossed it. Our omnibus groaned and rattled slowly up a bleak northern slope, among bald rocks, withered grass and still unbudded trees. It crossed the col and suddenly, as though by a miracle, the ground was yellow with innumerable primroses, each flower a little emblem of the sun that had called it into being.

And when at last one has arrived at San Sepolcro, what is there to be seen? A little town surrounded by walls, set in a broad flat valley between hills; some fine Renaissance palaces with pretty balconies of wrought iron; a not very interesting church, and finally, the best picture in the world.

The best picture in the world is painted in fresco on the wall of a room in the town hall. Some unwittingly beneficent vandal had it covered, some time after it was painted, with a thick layer of plaster, under which it lay hidden for a century or two, to be revealed at last in a state of preservation remarkably perfect for a fresco of its date. Thanks to the vandals, the visitor who now enters the Palazzo dei Conservatori at Borgo San Sepolcro finds the stupendous Resurrection almost as Piero della Francesca left it. Its clear, yet subtly sober colours shine out from the wall with scarcely impaired freshness. Damp has blotted out nothing of the design, nor dirt obscured it. We need no imagination to help us figure forth its beauty; it stands there before us in entire and actual splendour, the greatest picture in the world.

The greatest picture in the world. . . . You smile. The expression is ludicrous, of course. Nothing is more futile than the occupation of those connoisseurs who spend their time compiling first and second elevens of the world's best painters, eights and fours of musicians, fifteens of poets, all-star troupes of architects and so on. Nothing is so futile because there are a great many kinds of merit and an infinite variety of human beings. Is Fra Angelico a better artist than Rubens? Such questions, you insist, are meaningless. It is all a matter of personal taste. And up to a point this is true. But there does exist, none the less, an absolute standard of artistic merit. And it is a standard which is in the last resort a moral one. Whether a work of art is good or bad depends entirely on the quality of the character which expresses itself in the work. Not that all virtuous men are good artists, nor all artists conventionally virtuous. Longfellow was a bad poet, while Beethoven's dealings with his publishers were frankly dishonourable. But one can be dishonourable towards one's publishers and yet preserve the kind of virtue that is necessary to a good artist. That virtue is the virtue of integrity, of honesty towards oneself. Bad art is of two sorts: that which is merely dull, stupid and incompetent, the negatively bad; and the positively bad, which is a lie and a sham. Very often the lie is so well told that almost every one is taken in by it—for a time. In the end, however, lies are always found out. Fashion changes, the public learns to look with a different focus and, where a little while ago it saw an admirable work which actually moved its emotions, it now sees a sham. In the history of the arts we find innumerable shams of this kind, once taken as genuine, now seen to be false. The very names of most of them are now forgotten. Still, a dim rumour that Ossian once was read, that Bulwer was thought a great novelist and "Festus" Bailey a mighty poet still faintly reverberates. Their counterparts are busily earning praise and money at the present day. I often wonder if I am one of them. It is impossible to know. For one can be an artistic swindler without meaning to cheat and in the teeth of the most ardent desire to be honest.

Sometimes the charlatan is also a first-rate man of genius and then you have such strange artists as Wagner and Bernini, who can turn what is false and theatrical into something almost sublime.

That it is difficult to tell the genuine from the sham is proved by the fact that enormous numbers of people have made mistakes and continue to make them. Genuineness, as I have said, always triumphs in the long run. But at any given moment the majority of people, if they do not actually prefer the sham to the real, at least like it as much, paying an indiscriminate homage to both.

And now, after this little digression we can return to San Sepolcro and the greatest picture in the world. Great it is, absolutely great, because the man who painted it was genuinely noble as well as talented. And to me personally the most moving of pictures, because its author possessed almost more than any other painter those qualities of character which I most admire and because his purely aesthetic preoccupations are of a kind which I am by nature best fitted to understand. A natural, spontaneous and unpretentious grandeur—this is the leading quality of all Piero's work. He is majestic without being at all strained, theatrical or hysterical—as Handel is majestic, not as Wagner. He achieves grandeur naturally with every gesture he makes, never consciously strains after it. Like Alberti, with whose architecture, as I hope to show, his painting has certain affinities, Piero seems to have been inspired by what I may call the religion of Plutarch's *Lives*—which is not Christianity, but a worship of what is admirable in man. Even his technically religious pictures are paeans in praise of human dignity. And he is everywhere intellectual.

With the drama of life and religion he is very little concerned. His battle pictures at

Arezzo are not dramatic compositions in spite of the many dramatic incidents they contain. All the turmoil, all the emotions of the scenes have been digested by the mind into a grave intellectual whole. It is as though Bach had written the 1812 Overture. Nor are the two superb pictures in the National Gallery—the Nativity and the Baptism—distinguished for any particular sympathy with the religious or emotional significance of the events portrayed. In the extraordinary Flagellation at Urbino, the nominal subject of the picture recedes into the background on the left-hand side of the panel, where it serves to balance the three mysterious figures standing aloof in the right foreground. We seem to have nothing here but an experiment in composition, but an experiment so strange and so startlingly successful that we do not regret the absence of dramatic significance and are entirely satisfied. The Resurrection at San Sepolcro is more dramatic. Piero has made the simple triangular composition symbolic of the subject. The base of the triangle is formed by the sepulchre; and the soldiers sleeping round it are made to indicate by their position the upward jet of the two sides, which meet at the apex in the face of the risen Christ, who is standing, a banner in his right hand, his left foot already raised and planted on the brim of the sepulchre, preparing to set out into the world. No geometrical arrangement could have been more simple or more apt. But the being who rises before our eyes from the tomb is more like a Plutarchian hero than the Christ of conventional religion. The body is perfectly developed, like that of a Greek athlete; so formidably strong that the wound in its muscular flank seems somehow an irrelevance. The face is stern and pensive, the eyes cold. The whole figure is expressive of physical and intellectual power. It is the resurrection of the classical ideal, incredibly much grander and more beautiful than the classical reality, from the tomb where it had lain so many hundred years.

Aesthetically, Piero's work has this resemblance to Alberti's: that it too is essentially an affair of masses. What Alberti is to Brunelleschi, Piero della Francesca is to his contemporary, Botticelli. Botticelli was fundamentally a draughtsman, a maker of supple and resilient lines, thinking in terms of arabesques inscribed on the flat. Piero, on the contrary, has a passion for solidity as such. There is something in all his works that reminds one constantly of Egyptian sculpture. Piero has that Egyptian love of the smooth rounded surface that is the external symbol and expression of a mass. The faces of his personages look as though they were carved out of some very hard rock into which it had been impossible to engrave the details of a human physiognomy—the hollows, the lines and wrinkles of real life. They are ideal, like the faces of Egyptian gods and princes, surface meeting and marrying with curved unbroken surface in an almost geometrical fashion. Look, for example, at the faces of the woman in Piero's fresco at Arezzo: "The Queen of Sheba recognizing the Holy Tree." They are all of one peculiar cast: the foreheads are high, rounded and smooth; the necks are like cylinders of polished ivory; from the midst of the concave sockets the eyelids swell out in one uninterrupted curve into convexity; the cheeks are unbrokenly smooth, and the subtle curvature of their surfaces is indicated by a very delicate chiaroscuro which suggests more powerfully the solidity and mass of the flesh than the most spectacular Caravaggioesque light and shade could do.

Piero's passion for solidity betrays itself no less strikingly in his handling of the dresses and drapery of his figures. It is noticeable, for example, that wherever the subject permits, he makes his personages appear in curious head-dresses that remind one by their solid geometrical qualities of those oddly shaped ceremonial hats or tiaras worn by the statues of Egyptian kings. Among the frescoes at Arezzo are several which illustrate this peculiarity. In that representing Heraclius restoring the True Cross to Jerusalem, all the ecclesiastical dignitaries are wearing enormously high head-dresses, conical, trumpet-shaped, even rectangular. They are painted very smoothly with, it is obvious, a profound relish for their solidity. One or two similar head-dresses, with many varieties of wonderfully rounded helmets, are lovingly represented in the battle-pieces in the same place. The Duke of Urbino, in the well-known portrait at the Uffizi, is wearing a red cloth cap whose shape is somewhat like that of the "Brodrick" of the modern English soldier, but without the peak— a cylinder fitting round the head, topped by a projecting disk as the crown. Its smoothness and the roundness of its surfaces are emphasized in the picture. Nor does Piero neglect the veils of his female figures. Though transparent and of lawn, they hang round the heads of his women in stiff folds, as though they were made of steel. Among clothes he has a special fondness for pleated bodices and tunics. The bulge and recession of the pleated stuff fascinates him, and he likes to trace the way in which the fluted folds follow the curve of the body beneath. To drapery he gives, as we might expect, a particular weight and richness. Perhaps his most exquisite handling of drapery is to be seen in the altar-piece of the Madonna della Misericordia, which now hangs near the Resurrection in the town hall at San Sepolcro. The central figure in this picture, which is one of the earliest of Piero's extant works, represents the Virgin, standing, and stretching out her arms, so as to cover two groups of suppliants on either side with the folds of her heavy blue mantle. The mantle and the Virgin's dress hang in simple perpendicular folds, like the flutings on the robe of the archaic bronze charioteer at the Louvre. Piero has painted these alternately convex and concave surfaces with a peculiar gusto.

It is not my intention to write a treatise on Piero della Francesca; that has been done sufficiently often and sufficiently badly to make it unnecessary for me to bury that consummate artist any deeper under layers of muddy comment. All I have meant to do in this place is to give the reasons why I like his works and my justifications for calling the Resurrection the greatest picture in the world. I am attracted to his character by his intellectual power; by his capacity for unaffectedly making the grand and noble gesture; by his pride in whatever is splendid in humanity. And in the artist I find peculiarly sympathetic the lover of solidity, the painter of smooth curving surfaces, the composer who builds with masses. For myself I prefer him to Botticelli, so much so indeed, that if it were necessary to sacrifice all Botticelli's works in order to save the Resurrection, the Nativity, the Madonna della Misericordia and the Arezzo frescoes, I should unhesitatingly commit the Primavera and all the rest of them to the flames. It is unfortunate for Piero's reputation that his works should be comparatively few and in most cases rather difficult of access. With the exception of the Nativity and Baptism at the National Gallery, all the really important works of Piero are at Arezzo, San Sepolcro and Urbino. The portraits of the Duke and Duchess of Urbino with their respective triumphs, in the Uffizi, are charming and exceedingly "amusing"; but they do not represent Piero at his best. The altar-piece at Perugia and the Madonna with saints and donor at Milan are neither of them first-rate. The St. Jerome at Venice is goodish; so too is the damaged fresco of the Malatesta, at Rimini. The Louvre possesses nothing, and Germany can only boast of a study of archi-

tecture, inferior to that at Urbino. Anybody, therefore, who wants to know Piero
must go from London to Arezzo, San Sepolcro and Urbino. Now Arezzo is a boring
sort of town, and so ungrateful to its distinguished sons that there is no monument
within its walls to the divine Aretino. I deplore Arezzo; but to Arezzo, nevertheless,
you must go to see Piero's most considerable
works. From Arezzo you must make your
way to San Sepolcro, where the inn is only
just tolerable, and to which the means of
communication are so bad that, unless you
come in your own car, you are fairly compelled to stay there. And from San Sepolcro you must travel by 'bus for seven hours
across the Apennines to Urbino. Here, it is
true, you have not only two admirable Pieros
(the Flagellation and an architectural
scene), but the most exquisite palace in Italy
and very nearly a good hotel. Even on the
most wearily reluctant tourist Urbino imposes itself; there is no escaping it; it must
be seen. But in the case of Arezzo and San
Sepolcro there is no such moral compulsion.
Few tourists, in consequence, take the trouble
to visit them.

If the principal works of Piero were to
be seen in Florence, and those of Botticelli at
San Sepolcro, I do not doubt that the public

estimation of these two masters would be reversed. Artistic English spinsters would stand in rapturous contemplation before the story of the True Cross, instead of before the Primavera. Raptures depend largely upon the stars in Baedeker, and the stars are more freely distributed to works of art in accessible towns than to those in the inaccessible. If the Arena chapel were in the mountains of Calabria, instead of at Padua, we should all have heard a good deal less of Giotto.

But enough. The shade of Conxolus rises up to remind me that I am running into the error of those who measure merit by a scale of oddness and rarity.

BEAUTY IN 1920

To those who know how to read the signs of the times it will have become apparent, in the course of these last days and weeks, that the Silly Season is close upon us. Already—and this in July with the menace of three or four new wars grumbling on the thunderous horizon—already a monster of the deep has appeared at a popular seaside resort. Already Mr. Louis McQuilland has launched in the *Daily Express* a fierce onslaught on the younger poets of the Asylum. Already the picture-papers are more than half filled with photographs of bathing nymphs—photographs that make one understand the ease with which St. Anthony rebuffed his temptations. The newspapermen, ramping up and down like wolves, seek their prey wherever they may find it; and it was with a unanimous howl of delight that the whole Press went pelting after the hare started by Mrs. Asquith in a recent instalment of her autobiography. Feebly and belatedly, let me follow the pack.

Mrs. Asquith's denial of beauty to the daughters of the twentieth century has proved a god-sent giant gooseberry. It has necessitated the calling in of a whole host of skin-food specialists, portrait-painters and photographers to deny this far from soft impeachment. A great deal of space has been agreeably and inexpensively filled. Every one is satisfied—public, editors, skin-food specialists and all. But by far the most interesting contribution to the debate was a pictorial one, which appeared, if I remember rightly, in the *Daily News*. Side by side, on the same page, we were shown the photographs of three beauties of the eighteen-eighties and three of the nineteen-twenties. The comparison was most instructive. For a great gulf separates the two types of beauty represented by these two sets of photographs.

I remember in *If*, one of those charming conspiracies of E. V. Lucas and George Morrow, a series of parodied fashion-plates entitled "If Faces get any Flatter. Last year's standard, this year's Evening Standard." The faces of our living specimens of beauty have grown flatter with those of their fashion-plate sisters. Compare the types of 1880 and 1920. The first is steep-faced, almost Roman in profile; in the contemporary beauties the face has broadened and shortened, the profile is less noble, less imposing, more appealingly, more alluringly pretty. Forty years ago it was the aristocratic type that was appreciated; to-day the popular taste has shifted from the countess to the soubrette. Photography confirms the fact that the ladies of the 'eighties looked like Du Maurier drawings. But among the present young generation one looks in vain for the type; the Du Maurier damsel is as extinct as the mesozoic reptile; the Fish girl and other kindred flat-faced species have taken her place.

Between the 'thirties and 'fifties another type, the egg-faced girl, reigned supreme in the affections of the world. From the early portraits of Queen Victoria to the fashion-plates in the *Ladies' Keepsake* this invariable type prevails—the egg-shaped face, the sleek hair, the swan-like neck, the round, champagne-bottle shoulders. Compared with the decorous impassivity of the oviform girl our flat-faced fashion-plates are terribly abandoned and provocative. And because one expects so much in the way of respectability from these egg-faces of an earlier age, one is apt to be shocked when one sees them conducting themselves in ways that seem unbefitting. One thinks of that enchanting picture of Etty's, "Youth on the Prow and Pleasure at the Helm." The naiads are of the purest egg-faced type. Their hair is sleek, their shoulders slope and their faces are as impassive as blanks. And yet they have no clothes on. It is almost indecent; one imagined that the egg-faced type came into the world complete with flowing draperies.

It is not only the face of beauty that alters with the changes of popular taste. The champagne-bottle shoulders of the oviform girl have vanished from the modern fashion-plate and from modern life. The contemporary hand, with its two middle fingers held together and the forefinger and little finger splayed apart, is another recent product. Above all, the feet have changed. In the days of the egg-faces no fashion-plate had more than one foot. This rule will, I think, be found invariable. That solitary foot projects, generally in a strangely haphazard way as though it had nothing to do with a leg, from under the edge of the skirt. And what a foot! It has no relation to those provocative feet in Suckling's ballad:

> Her feet beneath her petticoat
> Like little mice stole in and out.

It is an austere foot. It is a small, black, oblong object like a tea-leaf. No living human being has ever seen a foot like it, for it is utterly unlike the feet of nineteen-twenty. To-day the fashion-plate is always a biped. The tea-leaf has been replaced by two feet of rich baroque design, curved and florid, with insteps like the necks of Arab horses. Faces may have changed shape, but feet have altered far more radically. On the text, "the feet of the young women," it would be possible to write a profound philosophical sermon.

And while I am on the subject of feet I would like to mention another curious phenomenon of the same kind, but affecting, this time, the standards of male beauty. Examine the pictorial art of the eighteenth century and you will find that the shape of the male leg is not what it was. In those days the calf of the leg was not a muscle that bulged to its greatest dimensions a little below the back of the knee, to subside, *decrescendo*, towards the ankle. No, in the eighteenth century the calf was an even crescent, with its greatest projection opposite the middle of the shin; the ankle, as we know it, hardly existed. This curious calf is forced upon one's attention by almost every minor picture-maker of the eighteenth century, and even by some of the great masters, as, for instance, Blake. How it came into existence I do not know. Presumably the crescent calf was considered, in the art schools, to approach more nearly to the Platonic Idea of the human leg than did the poor dis-

torted Appearance of real life. Personally,
I prefer my calves with the bulge at the top
and a proper ankle at the bottom. But then
I don't hold much with the *beau idéal*.

The process by which one type of beauty
becomes popular, imposes its tyranny for a
period and then is displaced by a dissimilar
type is a mysterious one. It may be that
patient historical scholars will end by discovering some law to explain the transforma-
tion of the Du Maurier type into the flat-face
type, the tea-leaf foot into the baroque foot,
the crescent calf into the normal calf. As
far as one can see at present, these changes
seem to be the result of mere hazard and
arbitrary choice. But a time will doubtless
come when it will be found that these
changes of taste are as ineluctably predeter-
mined as any chemical change. Given the
South African War, the accession of Edward
VII. and the Liberal triumph of 1906, it
was, no doubt, as inevitable that Du Maurier
should have given place to Fish as that zinc
subjected to sulphuric acid should break up
into $ZnSO_4 + H_2$. But we leave it to others
to formulate the precise workings of the law.

SINCERITY IN ART

IN a recently published volume on the commercial side of literature, Mr. Michael Joseph, the literary agent, discussed the Best Seller. What are the qualities that cause a book to sell like soap or breakfast food or Ford cars? It is a question the answer to which we should all like to know. Armed with that precious recipe, we should go to the nearest stationer's shop, buy a hundred sheets of paper for sixpence, blacken them with magical scribbles and sell them again for six thousand pounds. There is no raw material so richly amenable to treatment as paper. A pound of iron turned into watch springs is worth several hundreds or even thousands of times its original value; but a pound of paper turned into popular literature may be sold at a profit of literally millions per cent. If only we knew the secret of the process by which paper is turned into popular literature! But we don't. Even Mr. Joseph is ignorant. Otherwise, it is obvious, he would be writing Best Sellers, an occupation more profitable even than his present profession, which is selling them.

The only thing Mr. Joseph can tell us is

this: the Best Seller must be sincere.   The
information is quite true—so manifestly true,
indeed, that it is not particularly useful.
All literature, all art, best seller or worst,
must be sincere, if it is to be successful.   The
deliberate pastiche, be it of Charles Garvice
or of Shelley, can never take in any considerable number of people over any considerable
period of time.   A man cannot successfully
be anything but himself.   It is obvious.
Only a person with a Best Seller mind can
write Best Sellers; and only some one with
a mind like Shelley's can write *Prometheus
Unbound*.   The deliberate forger has little
chance with his contemporaries and none at
all with posterity.

In the annals of literary history, however,
there have been but few deliberate forgers.
There was the Elizabethan Greene, for example, who pastiched *Euphues* and forged
the poetical style of Marlowe, in the hope of
securing for himself some of the popular applause which greeted the appearance of
Lyly's novels and Marlowe's plays.   His
own style, when he wrote in it, was an agreeable and charming one.   His borrowed
plumes are a manifest misfit and can never
have impressed any one.

Another and more recent literary man who
attained a considerable celebrity by forging

and pastiching was the Frenchman, Catulle Mendès. Reading his horribly clever second-hand works one is astonished now that they took in as many people as they did. His gold is so obviously pinch-beck, his jewels such palpable stage copies of the real gems. It is difficult to be interested in such people. Their work has little or nothing to do with art, and their unmysterious personality raises no curious or subtle problems of psychology. They are the literary counterpart of the people who fake Sienese Primitives or Chippendale chairs for profit; that is all. The only kind of insincere art that is worthy of the psychologist's attention is that which is insincere, not deliberately, but unwittingly and in spite of the efforts of the artist to be sincere.

In the affairs of ordinary life sincerity is a matter of will. We can be sincere or insincere at choice. It may seem, therefore, a paradox when I talk of works of art that are insincere in spite of their author's desires and efforts to make them sincere. If he wants to be sincere, it may be argued, he can be; there is nothing to prevent him but his own lack of goodwill. But this is not true. Sincerity in art depends on other things besides the mere desire to be sincere.

It would be easy to adduce many examples

of artists whose works have been insincere, in spite of the fact that they themselves have been, in life, perfect models of sincerity. There is, for instance, the case of Benjamin Robert Haydon, the friend of Keats and Shelley, the painter of some of the largest and most pretentious religious pictures ever executed. His autobiography—one of the best books of its kind, which the stupidity of publishers has permitted to remain out of print for the last fifty years—exists to testify to the man's sincerity in life, to his spontaneous ardours, his genuinely noble idealism, his numerous and not unlovable failings. But look at his pictures—the pictures to which he devoted a lifetime of passionate endeavour. Look at them—that is, if you can find any to look at; for they are mostly in the cellars beneath our galleries, not on the walls. They are full of stage grandeur, the cold convention of passion, the rhetorical parody of emotion. They are "insincere"— the word comes inevitably to the lips.

The same dramatic contrast between the man and his works can be found in the Belgian painter Wiertz, whose studio at Brussels draws more visitors than does the city's picture gallery—but draws, not because the painter's pictures are moving works of art, but because they are monstrosities of size and melodramatic horror. This dreamer of Michelangelesque dreams survives as a sort of pictorial Barnum; his museum has the popularity of a Chamber of Horrors.

Alfieri was another of these sincere and thoroughly genuine human beings who produce an art that is insincere and stagey. It is difficult to believe that the Autobiography and the wooden, stilted, conventional tragedies were written by the same man.

The truth is that sincerity in art is not an affair of will, of a moral choice between honesty and dishonesty. It is mainly an affair of talent. A man may desire with all his soul to write a sincere, a genuine book and yet lack the talent to do it. In spite of his sincere intentions, the book turns out to be unreal, false and conventional; the emotions are stagily expressed, the tragedies are pretentious and lying shams, and what was meant to be dramatic is baldly melodramatic. Reading, the critic is chilled and disgusted. He pronounces the book to be "insincere." The author, conscious of the purity of his intentions when he wrote it, is outraged by an epithet which seems to impugn his honour and his sense of moral values, but which, in reality, stigmatizes only his intellectual capacities. For in matters of art "being sincere" is synonymous with "possessing the gifts of psychological understanding and expression."

All human beings feel very much the same emotions; but few know exactly what they feel or can divine the feelings of others. Psychological insight is a special faculty, like the faculty for understanding mathematics or music. And of the few who possess that faculty only two or three in every hundred are born with the talent of expressing their knowledge in artistic form. Let us take an obvious example. Many people—most people, perhaps—have been at one time or another violently in love. But few have known how to analyse their feelings, and fewer still have been able to express them. The love letters that are read aloud in the divorce courts and at the inquests on romantic suicides prove how pathetically inept as literary artists most men and women are. They feel, they suffer, they are inspired by a sincere emotion; but they cannot write. Stilted, conventional, full of stock phrases and time-worn rhetorical tropes, the average love letter of real life would be condemned, if read in a book, as being in the last degree "insincere." I have read genuine letters written by suicides just before their death, which I should, as a reviewer, have pilloried for their manifest "insincerity." And yet, after all, it would be difficult to demand of a man a higher proof of the sincerity of his emotions than that which he furnishes by killing himself because of them. Only suicides of talent write letters that are artistically "sincere." The rest, incapable of expressing what they feel, are compelled to fall back on the trite, "insincere" rhetoric of the second-rate novel.

It is the same with love letters. We read the love letters of Keats with a passionate interest; they describe in the freshest and most powerful language the torments of a soul that is conscious of every detail of its agony. Their "sincerity" (the fruit of their author's genius) renders them as interesting, as artistically important as Keats's poems; more important even, I sometimes think. Imagine, now, the love letters of any other young apothecary's assistant of the same epoch! He might have been as hopelessly in love as was Keats with Fanny Brawne. But his letters would be worthless, uninteresting, painfully "insincere." We should find their slightly superior counterpart in any of the long-forgotten sentimental novels of the period.

We should, therefore, be very chary of applying the epithet "insincere" to a work of art. Only those works are insincere in the true, the ethical sense of the word, which are—like Greene's, like Catulle Mendès's—deliberate forgeries and conscious pastiches. Most of the works which we label as "insincere" are in reality only incompetent, the product of minds lacking in the (for the artist) indispensable gifts of psychological understanding and expression.

THE END